JUST A
Step

The Autobiography of
LEANNE
GROSE

GreenUmbrella
Publishing

This edition first published in the UK in 2008
By Green Umbrella Publishing

© Green Umbrella Publishing 2008

www.justastep.co.uk

Publishers: Jules Gammond and Vanessa Gardner

Creative Director: Kevin Gardner

Picture Credits: Leanne Grose, CameraCraft and Damon Taylor

The right of Leanne Grose and Claire Welch to be identified as authors of
this book have been asserted by them in accordance with the Copyright,
Designs and Patents Act 1988.

Printed and bound by J. H. Haynes & Co. Ltd., Sparkford

ISBN: 978-1-906229-47-4

In the darkest times you meet the kindest of angels.

LEANNE GROSE

This book is dedicated to the people that fuel my heart and keep me smiling – my darling family and amazing friends. To the nurses and those who have wiped my tears, the physiotherapists who have held my hand and to the friends I've lost along the way.

Finally, this is for my granny who took a part of me when she died.

I'll always love you and hope you're proud.

Contents

Introduction

How can I only be 26 years old and writing a book about my life, you might ask? I've asked myself that same question over and over but, the truth is, that over the past six years, I've had one crazy journey. There have been ups, which include meeting the most amazing people from the world of showbiz and business, as well as those who have stories like mine. But, there have also been many downs, where I've met people who have literally been to hell and back.

I never expected to be diagnosed with a rare form of cancer at the age of 20 but, when I was, it became the start of some exciting events as well as the cause of a great deal of heartache. After radiotherapy and various other treatments failed me, I faced losing the lower part of my left leg. My foot had become pretty useless and at the time, despite it being a devastating blow, I thought it would be for the best. After a number of major operations I set out to improve my quality of life. In a surprise twist of fate, an amazing chain of events began to unfold and I hope as a result, that one day, I might be the first amputee to make

it down a red carpet on crutches turning each and every negative into something positive. There are many tales to tell.

This is my story.

JUST A *Step*

Chapter 1

To begin at the beginning

I do look at my life as a whole and think how lucky I have
been. I was born Leanne Louise Grose, the first child of
Kevin and Gail Grose, on 5 February 1981 at Treliske
Hospital in Truro, now called the Royal Cornwall Hospital.
My parents have been in love since my mum was only 12
years old and my dad was 15, and I grew up in an
extremely loving environment where I felt blessed. Two
years and two days after my own birth, Chris, or Chrissy as
I often call him, my gorgeous brother arrived, and our
family was complete. My childhood was fun and
adventurous and my parents took us on trips, we would
play in the park and life was good. I was also happy and
content with my own company and I always enjoyed
reading and writing, especially poetry. I found, at any early
age, that I loved school and I went to the local primary
and junior school, St Dennis, where I was lucky enough to
be picked for all the sports teams and I found myself in

the top set for academic subjects.

I couldn't be described as a "geek" or a "swot" but I just enjoyed school for what it was and I loved to learn. I had two amazing teachers, Mr Walker and Mr Lane, who both inspired me while I respected them. They gave me incentive and both had wonderful voices that were full of character and enchantment which meant I loved to sit and listen to their stories. My mind was regularly swept into a world of imagination during their classes. Their belief in me was completely inspiring and they drove me because I wanted them to be proud.

Now, those who know me will tell you I'm no shrinking violet and never have been. From a young age I was always someone who thrived on being the centre of attention and I had an excitable group of friends, including Donna, Chantelle, Lisa, Kay, Kelly, Vicky and Laura and I was never taunted or bullied at school. This same group of friends also lived near me so it was friendship in the playground and water fights at weekends. A special day in the year was always sports day. I felt so proud sitting on the school sports field waiting to compete while knowing that my parents would be there happy and smiling, always

cheering me on. I took up running cross-country with Donna. She was my next door neighbour and we looked so alike that people were always mistaking us for sisters. We did virtually everything together. We were chosen to represent the school and although I found the challenging courses tough, I'll never forget the day that my dad slipped £5 in my pocket for doing well at an event. I felt rich. Running was fun, but nothing compared to my true passion, netball. The adrenaline was pumping as I put on my trainers and "bib" and took up my position as goal attack. I loved the thrill of the game. I loved taking charge and always played to win.

As well as wonderful parents and my brother I also have the love of a big family. My dad was one of four children and so there are aunties, uncles and cousins as well as his parents, gran and gramps. Christmas time was always fun and parties were something else! My mum has a sister, Elaine, and then there is my uncle and my cousin Amy. My granny, my maternal grandmother, was someone immensely special to me. She always made me feel loved and I adored her. My granny had not had an easy life and was adopted at a young age when both her parents died.

Granny was lucky to be adopted by a wonderful family and she gained a new sister, Auntie Ciss. Later, Auntie Ciss married Bryce – who became like a father to my mum – and Auntie Ciss had a daughter, Carole, who is my wonderful godmother. Granny was family oriented and when she lost both her husbands to cancer and leukaemia while she was still young, she brought up Elaine and Gail and then threw herself wholeheartedly into being a grandmother. Chris, Amy and I were always doted on by her. I felt deeply loved by this woman and I, in turn, had so much love and respect for her. I looked up to her, and even when I was young, everyone could clearly see the similarities between us – there was the wild temper and stubbornness for a start. She lived close by and I would pop in every day to see her on the way to or from school. I loved spending time with her and she would often give me 50 pence for some sweets. If Chris and I stayed with her overnight, she would throw herself into any game that we wanted to play. Weddings and shops were always popular and she would let us stay up late while she "served at the till" or laughed at me as I walked down the imaginary aisle with her net curtains placed

strategically on my head.

Although I had a great childhood, I think you only appreciate how amazing it all is when you are older and all the little things begin to mean so much. We were one of the first families in our area to go abroad on holiday. We weren't rich by any stretch of the imagination, but mum and dad worked hard and wanted us to experience as much as we could of the big wide world. First foreign destination: Majorca. The only problem was my new-found fear – flying! I sat on the plane, just 12 years old, absolutely petrified. Although mum and dad didn't show it, I knew they were scared too and we all sat side by side holding hands. Chris, meanwhile, bounded round the plane as if nothing could be more exciting. Why didn't anything frighten him? Was I the baby of the family after all? I put my head down as we took off and closed my eyes. I prayed. I prayed that we'd be safe and that my family would come to no harm. I was never particularly religious, but I did go to Sunday school – mainly to take part in the sports clubs and the plays, and my mum liked to dress me up and enjoy a quiet Sunday morning while I was out. I actually did, however, believe and at the time I was praying

on the plane, I wholeheartedly believed as my knuckles got whiter by the second. I don't know exactly why I was so desperately scared. I think perhaps it was because my family were with me and I couldn't bear the fact that anything could happen to them. Don't get me wrong – I'm no hero – but I have always loved them more than myself, even when I was young. Majorca was fabulous and we swam, played, laughed and ate our way through the holiday. I loved being in another country and found the Spanish way of life fascinating. I loved listening to the language as I ploughed my way through so much ice cream every night that I thought I was going to be sick. Apart from the flying, the holiday was one of the best times in my childhood. On a scale of 1 to 10, life was right up there and days would drift by filled with laughter and fun. Life was carefree.

I moved from junior school to senior school, where I attended Brannel Secondary, and revelled in the change. There were even more friends to make and I was soon part of the "in-crowd" of girls. Lessons were fun and I felt I was growing as a person. As well as the comfort of my routine, I enjoyed being a girl, living life and I started to

get an eye for the boys.

So that's the first chapter of my life – all in all a great start – I had a happy childhood. I was finding my feet.

But adolescent years weren't always so joyful, especially when one day my first health disaster took hold. I had a terrible headache one evening and an aching pain down one side of my neck. It wasn't particularly nice, but I passed it off as "one of those things" and decided to get some much needed sleep. I crept into bed feeling a little sorry for myself. The following morning when my parents' alarm went off in the next room I heard my mum stir. As usual she popped into my brother's room and then mine to give us the traditional: "Morning darling...time to get up, you don't want to be late for school" chorus, but as she entered my room something was different. She could clearly see something was wrong, meanwhile, I could only feel it. The ache in my head and neck were still present but had increased and the pain, by this time, had spread to my face.

It was more of an ache I suppose than a pain, but it was severe and unknown. As I got up out of bed and moved over to my mirrored wardrobes I gasped in horror.

What on earth was wrong with me? One side of my face had totally "dropped". I turned to my mum and I tried to speak, but the words I wanted to shout out didn't come. Mum threw her arms around me – she was worried and as always extremely loving – and hugged me protectively as I tried to talk. The words that came out were mumbled and dribble fell from my limp mouth. I couldn't even cry properly as my left eye wouldn't close and I felt very frustrated that I couldn't communicate how sad and scared I felt inside. I dressed quickly in the race to the doctor where I hoped he could fix what I felt was my "broken and horrific face". Was it a stroke? Had I had some bad reaction to something? These and other questions formed in my mind as my mum wrapped me in a red scarf and coat. I discovered quickly that I couldn't do the smallest things. I couldn't blink – which sounds strange – and it is only when you can't do something that you realise that you take it for granted and understand just how important it seems to be. My eye just continued to run and however hard I tried to close it I couldn't. My speech was appalling and I simply mumbled, slurred my words and dribbled like a baby. What was worse was that I couldn't smile. Was I

going to be like this forever? The thought terrified me.

Although it was summer, mum had wrapped my face snugly into a scarf in an attempt to protect it from any wind there might be. As we passed the village shop on the way to the doctor, a boy from school shouted: "Why is she wearing that scarf? It's not winter you know." It was obvious that mum was scared when she ran over to him and began shouting at him that I wasn't well. The fact that she was frightened made the panic inside me even worse. When we arrived at the doctor's surgery I had a feeling that it was all going to be okay. After all, wasn't that what the doctor was for – to make everything better again? I suppose I was lucky that I had been generally well and fit and had never really had to visit the doctor apart from when I once tripped during a school rounders match. I broke a bone in my wrist and after the initial pain, got to wear a trendy plaster cast for six weeks which I paraded at school as if it were a medal. My dad called me a drama queen – where on earth could he have got that idea from?

Anyway, back to the more serious matter of my face resembling something out of a horror movie. "Leanne", the receptionist called when it was my turn to see the

doctor. My mum took my hand and we went into the consulting room for the all important verdict. "Umm", he said as he looked into my staring watery eye while his cold hand touched my neck. He spoke again: "Definitely not a stroke". Mum looked relieved and I felt it – I didn't even know that you could have a stroke that young. He looked in a book and raised his head to say that in his opinion I had something called Bell's palsy. We had never heard of it before and all I wanted to know was how long it would take before this hideous ache would go and when would I be back to my normal worry-free self? The doctor sent me home with a large amount of steroids having told mum and me that he had no idea how long it would last but not to expect it to disappear overnight. He said it could have been caused by some sort of chill, oh, and he also said that it was very rare in someone my age. But, that was me. Unique!

I hated taking the pills. They'd get halfway down my throat and I'd feel like I was choking. With a fair amount of drama, gulping what felt like gallons of water, I'd cry like a baby as I tried to cough them back up. The steroids were tiny, in actual fact, and "tablet time" was something

I would have to get used to if I wanted to look normal again. It was a real ordeal but eventually after many tears and quite a few tantrums I decided to just get on with taking the pills and tablet time became a much quieter affair. It was just as well I changed my attitude and made the process easier all round as I had to take the tablets for a very long time. It felt like an age before I got better, in fact, it was six months and I did everything I was told. As I sat watching television I'd massage my face to try and stimulate it desperately trying to raise my mouth back to where it should be and to get everything working again. I spent most of that summer indoors which was incredibly frustrating. I was always the "class clown", but I was used to people laughing with me and I couldn't bear the thought of them laughing at me.

I didn't go out and join my friends in their water fights and I would only allow close friends in to see me. Even when I did, I would cover the side of my face with my hand to hide it. But, every cloud has a silver lining, as they say, and mum who was working at the village shop at the time would come home each day with get well cards and boxes of chocolates from well-wishers. It seemed to "sweeten"

the pain somewhat and all in all as time progressed, my face slowly returned to normal. I could flash my cheeky smile and life was good again.

I'm just grateful that I didn't have a crystal ball that could show me how much my life would soon change forever.

JUST A *Step*

Chapter 2

Running with laughter

As a crazy young teenager, memories of the droopy face and sloppy smile faded. At last, I was back to discos, dancing and dating and life was definitely great again. I found some sense of worth, when aged 14, I became a babysitter for a young family that lived near me. The two gorgeous little boys that I looked after, Ross and Jason, were certainly little bundles of fun and they managed to keep me on my toes. But I soon took a job in the popular seaside town of Newquay where the best thing was working with my best friend, Nathan. Although I was quite young for the job, with Nathan there I wasn't on my own and my parents had thought it would give me some independence. They had always been keen for me to value money and Chris and I were brought up to work hard and appreciate what we had in life. It turned out to be one of the best summers ever where I worked in the Italian restaurant Macaris. As well as being a restaurant, Macaris was also an

ice-cream parlour in the middle of the town where life was certainly buzzing.

The tourists, nightlife and general atmosphere were exciting and I began to feel quite grown up. My first pay packet certainly helped to fuel my journey to adulthood and I felt so proud of that little brown envelope full of crisp hard-earned notes. I remember desperately wanting to get home that day so that I could share my elation with my family. I was so excited by my new-found wealth that I treated the whole family to fish and chips for tea.

Each morning, Nathan and I would jump on a double-decker bus heading for our summer jobs and we would spend the journey chatting and gossiping. Like Donna, Nathan was my neighbour. He lived three doors away and we became incredibly close. We were very similar and both loved singing and acting and were generally flamboyant and outgoing. They were carefree days filled with meeting new people and striking up new friendships. But, the manager of Macaris was far from stupid, and decided that it might be better to split Nathan and me up during working hours. We were two typical teenagers with summer jobs and we were more likely to do some work if

we couldn't chat to each other all day. He suggested that I work in an ice-cream kiosk situated close to the beach. Despite leaving Nathan behind in the restaurant, the move to the kiosk was fabulous. I felt like my own boss and it enabled me to take my school revision where I read through my work while munching my way through the fudge sticks and flakes!

The move to the kiosk was also good for my confidence and I loved to watch the tourists milling about, enjoying their holiday, arguing or walking back from the beach burnt and sore. As I served whippy ice creams and chatted to the customers, I was also watching the crowds and the action going on around me. I could sit watching and daydreaming for hours. It was my responsibility to take the cash back to the boss at the end of each day – along with any remaining fudge sticks, of course. A new member of staff joined Macaris who started working alongside Nathan. When I met Andrew I was my usual chatty self and I don't think being chatty has ever done me any harm. Nathan and I decided that we would go out one night and spend some of the hard-earned cash that had been burning a hole in our pockets all summer.

We were far too young for Newquay's nightclubs, but that wasn't going to stop us blowing off some steam. We invited another friend, Chantelle, to join us and we raced home to get dressed up for our big night out on the tiles. Nathan decided to play matchmaker and he also invited Andrew to come out with us. Feeling very grown up, I was excited as I got ready in my bedroom. I knew I'd have to look 18 if I was to stand a chance of making it into any of the trendy clubs. Nathan and his mum, Sue, picked me up while my mum was busy giving me the "pep" talk about what we should and shouldn't be doing on our night out. I suppose the fact that I was growing up must have been strange for them and Newquay was, and still is, pretty renowned for its wild, and occasionally, violent reputation. As Sue drove I was buzzing. I felt incredibly grown up in my slinky black top and short lilac skirt.

Sue dropped us off and Nathan, Chantelle and I met with Andrew and headed for our first destination. We chose a popular nightclub for locals and tourists alike in the centre of town. The bouncers obviously spotted us coming a mile off. We tried casually walking up the steps to the entrance and were met by a burly man in black.

"Any ID?" he grunted. We tried to play it cool and look like typical 18-year-olds, but as the pressure for us to come clean mounted, I simply started giggling and we all ran off. Yes, not very mature and maybe a bit childish, but I suppose that's what you get when you're 14 and trying to lie about your age. We tried a few other clubs where we all took it in turns to go first at facing the ever inquisitive "bulldogs" at the door of each venue. Just as we were about to give up hope, call it a night and settle for a burger instead of a beer we got lucky at the last place we tried. Steamers opened its doors to Chantelle and me as we turned on the innocent charm. We glided through the entrance. We'd done it! Yes, four 14-year-olds had got in and we were all chuffed with our victory.

We played it cool and headed for a table trying to blend in. We bought drinks – alcoholic, of course – and began our evening of fun. It soon became obvious to me that Nathan and Chantelle were trying to get Andrew and me together. I wasn't keen on the idea to begin with as I'd always been shy around boys – especially if I liked them. But, fuelled with illegal alcohol, I attempted to chat to him. It soon became apparent that Andrew was as shy

around girls as I was around boys. The difference was that he didn't become less shy as the alcohol flowed so I did that thing you do when you're 14 years old and drinking and I went straight for Nathan. Yes, I know, we were best friends and we were crossing a line that perhaps we shouldn't but, we were very young, in need of fun and we went from sharing gossip and lunch breaks to sharing saliva. The evening rounded off a great summer – it's certainly one that neither Nathan, nor I, will forget – and we found ourselves back in the classroom revising for exams. As for my best friend and I, we went back to being exactly that – just best friends. Just the way it was meant to be.

From a quick summer fling with Nathan I launched into my first proper romance. It was with someone in my year at school called Michael. Obviously, being at school together, we'd known each other a while and strange as it may seem, it was perfectly natural to move our friendship from being classmates to stolen kisses on the school field and holding hands under the table in maths class. I'd been aware that Michael had liked me for a couple of years, but the tomboy in me had been more into building camps

than going out with someone. Also, there was always something that held me back from talking to boys because I always felt embarrassed. While I was always confident with my friends and loved being a "performer" I was like a wilting flower when it came to the opposite sex.

Going back a little, my first encounter with someone I liked was with Matt. He was older than me and my whole world seemed to revolve around him. I swore to my friends it was love – maybe not on his part – but it definitely was on mine. Maybe I watched too many romantic "chick flicks", or enjoyed listening to my friends' tales of love and lust at the weekly disco. Whatever it was, there was something about Matt which could make my stomach flip. At school, break times were like landmines. Was he looking at me? Was my hair looking good? Was I smiling enough? Oh, the pain of teenage angst. He was well aware that I liked him and more and more he would come over to say hello. But I would freeze every time he did and I suddenly lost the power of speech. What was wrong with me? My witty banter would fail me as I turned into a mumbling wreck.

The weekly disco was held in the local football club

and one night I knew Matt would be there. I wasn't taking any chances, so wearing my best outfit and armed with my biggest smile I entered the disco ready to make something happen. I sat with my friends at a table near to where he was sat where I could see and hear him laughing and joking with his mates. I was hoping that he would look over and see the "real" me, but as I turned to see if he was looking at me I spotted him chatting to another girl. That was it. He doesn't even like me, I thought to myself, and I ran off to the toilets with my girlfriends in tow ready for a pow-wow. Like a coven of witches we clung together reviewing what had just happened while we also discussed who each of my friends had their own eyes on too. They were sympathetic and knew how much I liked Matt. After all, he was all I had rambled on about for the past couple of years. It was typical teenage drama.

Just then, like out of the movies, the door was flung open and in what seemed like slow motion, there stood Matt. He was looking at me – yes, me – and he reached out his hand and grasped mine. I swear to you, my heart skipped a beat and he said nothing as he led me back to the disco and onto the dance floor. It was like a dream and

my embarrassment faded as he put his arms around my trembling body as we danced to "The Power Of Love" by Jennifer Rush. I'll never forget that song. I'll never forget that dance and I'll never forget that night. But, as the song ended, so did my nerve and instead of waiting for and, accepting a kiss, I simply held him close and lost all courage. It was the end of the night for me and he kissed me on the cheek as we said goodnight. It must have been the "love mist" in front of my eyes which made me forget my coat. As I entered the building again in search of it, I was hoping that maybe, just maybe, I'd get a glimpse of him once again. I found my coat and as I turned around I saw him. He had his back to me but as the crowd parted he was clearer to see and I could see he was kissing someone else – my close friend Lisa.

My heart felt as though it had been smashed into a million tiny pieces. How could he do that to me? How could she do that to me? I left the disco and raced home with tears in my eyes. I was heartbroken. At the time, it seemed like the biggest trauma in the world, although obviously, I've since learnt that it definitely wasn't. One day, I would meet Matt again and karma would prevail.

Petty trivia, such as Matt kissing my close friend, would soon fade into insignificance.

Very early one morning, a few days before Christmas, Chris was eating his breakfast while mum, dad and I were still all upstairs getting ready for the day. "Mum", Chris shrieked upstairs. "There's been an accident in the village and it's on TV". My world was about to flip. You just know sometimes when something is wrong and I felt a shiver run down my back. The next thing was Donna's mum knocking on the door. "It's Stephen", she cried, "Stephen's been killed."

Stephen was my dear friend. We sat together in science class and he had been with me through childhood and school. I sat on the stairs hardly taking in that my friend, aged just 15, had been killed in a car accident. Christmas was naturally a quiet time as I mourned him. Stephen's was the first funeral I had been to and I tried to be strong. The rest of my friends and I held each other close as we all wept quietly and said goodbye to our cherished friend. In the background, "Simply The Best" rang out true and loud. You reassess life when something sad and traumatic hits you and I felt that our tight-knit group at school

became closer. We no longer wanted to take each other for granted. So, it was a huge blow, when just eight weeks later, we received some more devastating news.

It was my dad's birthday and I heard mum on the phone. I knew something was wrong – sometimes you can't explain it – your heart just knows. As she hung up the phone my mum burst into uncontrollable tears and Chris and I both raced to be with her. "Bryce has passed away", she said. Bryce had been like a father to mum and he had taken her butterfly catching with jam jars and she had enjoyed spending a childhood of sitting in her uncle's bright red Mini. He'd been just as good to Chris and me and we'd spent hours listening to his fascinating stories. He was a gentle, kind man whom we all loved very much, and we all thought the world of him. I started to question how I'd gone from having a protected, carefree, perfect life, to losing two people I loved in just two months. I wasn't sure if I'd ever make sense of it.

Life doesn't stand still and exams came and went without too much stress and I began to feel that the two devastating events were beginning to mould me into a stronger person. It was around this time that my

relationship with Michael was beginning to flourish. My friends all had boyfriends and they all thought I should take a chance. So I did.

Michael was my first proper boyfriend and I was his first proper girlfriend. We enjoyed each other's company and had a great time having fun. We already knew each other's parents so we didn't have that embarrassment to get over and everything felt just right. As the days drifted by, our relationship was moving forward. With exams over, Nathan and I had gone back to our summer jobs and once again, life was carefree and easy. The only stress we had was which parties should we go to and how would we get there? Then, without any warning, I had that first night with Michael – a lot of my friends had been there already – and I changed from being a child into reaching my adulthood. I'd imagined that the first time you had sex it would be filled with fear, mystery and intrigue. Okay, so there weren't exactly fireworks and explosions – which is what I'd been expecting, promised by passionate characters in slushy movies – but it wasn't bad either and it happened with someone I liked. In time, it would only get better, and we seemed to spend day after day in a

permanent lip-lock. Outsiders might have said that we weren't that well suited. Michael was quiet and shy, while I still loved meeting people and making new friends. But, somehow we clicked.

Romance wasn't the only thing on my mind and I managed to tear myself away from Michael long enough to go for my first big interview. With the money I had saved from my summer job I bought myself a new suit. It wasn't particularly expensive, but I felt like a million dollars. There is something about a suit that made me feel I had an air of authority and importance and it certainly gave me the extra confidence I needed when I was interviewed by Dominique, the Head of Legal Services for Carrick District Council. My insides were shaking, but I firmly held my hand to hers. I was feeling a little intimidated as the position I was applying for was as a trainee within the local authority's legal department. The legal profession wasn't something I had ever thought about going into, but the excitement enveloped me when I found out that the job was mine. "A job for life", beamed my parents when they heard the news.

I slipped into the role with ease, kept my head down

and worked really hard. I was keen to impress my new employer and I made myself indispensable. For me, talking to staff at all levels came naturally and within a few months I was offered a pay rise. Things were working out perfectly and I couldn't wait to go home and share my news with mum and dad each day with tales of what I'd done and achieved. Then came another massive milestone – I passed my driving test. Admittedly, it was the third time I'd taken it but I couldn't have cared less – nothing could wipe the huge grin from my face – and I was thrilled. That same evening, my parents bought me my very first car. It was a red Fiesta which I decided to name Beryl (don't ask me why) and I adored driving myself about and being able to travel to work to a job that I loved.

My relationship with Michael was still ongoing, but I began to feel that my fledgling career was taking centre stage. I wanted to talk to Michael about my job but he just didn't seem interested. He had got himself a job as a builder and I was proud of him but when it came to me he didn't really want to know what I was up to. I had begun to mix with a variety of different people who came from all sorts of backgrounds and I lapped up my new world. It

seemed to be a world that Michael didn't want to be a part of and then one day my hand was forced over my floundering relationship.

The Tall Ships were docked in Falmouth and I'd volunteered to do some extra work at the big event. Carrick had a "do" and I found myself working in the beer tent – where I had the opportunity to meet a wider circle of colleagues from various departments. It was a glorious day and the sun was beating down on the beautiful Tall Ships as they sat in the harbour. I'd met a lot of people that day but there was one in particular that grabbed my attention. His name was Paul and I knew he was a manager in the housing department. We chatted for a while and he told me he was 19 years old and lived in Truro. From the instant that I met him I knew there was something intoxicating about him. Even though he was a stranger he made me laugh and he came across as mature and intelligent which I found made him all the more alluring and attractive. The event finally ended and, sadly, so did our day of flirting.

I found that I had a new strained attitude towards Michael and I'd be lying if I said it had nothing to do with

meeting Paul. I felt as if my work had opened up a different world for me than the one I shared with Michael, and what we had seemed to be repetitive and mundane. As time went by I told myself that Michael and I could work it out, but his continuing lack of interest in me, my job and my new friends became more evident and the cracks that had lain on the surface were beginning to widen. A few weeks later I was invited to a "thank you" meal which was laid on by Carrick for all those who had helped at the Tall Ships weekend. Michael made it clear that he didn't want to go so I arranged to go with Tina who I worked with. We arrived at our table and I looked over to see Paul. I couldn't help myself and I began flirting with him again. We found that we got on really well and although I felt that we were probably very different I felt hugely attracted to him. As the evening progressed, so did my confidence which was probably aided by the glass or two that I'd had to drink. I found out a number of things about this new friend. He wasn't 19 years old at all. He was actually 32 and was 15 years older than me. This may have put some people off, but for me, it was even more attractive. What I did find a little off-putting though was the fact that he had

been married and was now divorced. I think I found it difficult because I'd spent my life wrapped in a protective blanket and divorce was a new concept for me. But, I loved Paul's incredible spirit and amazing sense of fun and although there could be a huge issue over the age gap, I felt that I'd met my match on many levels.

That night, Paul was never far from my mind and I dreamt of him. But, as the drink wore off I awoke to face the guilt which got worse as I started to become more and more friendly with this intoxicating older man. It was time to face the music. Not many days later I drove home from work and went straight to Michael's house where I was determined to "do the right thing". As soon as I walked through the door I could tell he was in a bad mood. But, far from being upset, I found that I actually felt relieved. His mood was going to make it easier, if anything. "Let's go out", I offered, moving towards the door and my car. I didn't want us to have our conversation in earshot of Michael's parents. He followed me and I was unusually quiet as I went over what I was going to say to him. "Michael", I started. I wanted to be as gentle as possible but I came out with all the "old" excuses like: "I feel we've

grown apart." "It's not you, it's me." I finished with: "I still want to be friends", but he changed from being moody, to sad and then finally he was angry. Nothing seemed to calm him down and he jumped out of the car and just started to run. I decided to chase after him. I still worried about him and I hated the fact that I had made him so upset. We eventually both got back in the car and talked for what seemed like hours. He calmed down and we hugged goodbye. I wanted to know he was safe, so I watched as he walked back into his house.

I wasn't proud of my actions but my heart instantly told my head that I'd done the right thing. I was about to start a new, fresh and exciting chapter in my life and the next few weeks were almost surreal. I'd completely fallen for Paul and we spent all the free time we had getting to know one another. We snuggled up to watch films and I felt like a child and an adult all rolled into one. The time we spent together convinced me it was right to split from Michael and build a relationship with Paul. I had never known a relationship like this before. But, it wasn't going to be all plain sailing. For a start, this 32-year-old man had yet to meet my parents. When I met Paul's parents, Trina and

Peter, they took me in with open arms. They instantly made me feel like a part of their family and they seemed pleased that Paul and I were so happy.

I think in the beginning, my new relationship must have been hard for my parents, especially my dad. There wasn't a huge difference in age between dad and Paul and although dad really liked him, he still wasn't happy about me going out with an older man. But, he soon realised how much I felt for Paul and he trusted in my judgement that I was doing the right thing. Paul eventually became a part of our family and they weren't disappointed with my choice. It wasn't long, however, before I had actually moved in with Paul and our relationship went from strength to strength. We were blissfully happy and Paul turned out to be a real romantic who would often surprise me with flowers at work along with beautiful poetry and cards. He made me feel special.

I too, was a romantic. I always have been and I love planning birthday and Christmas surprises. We began to try to outdo each other on the romantic front which only added to the relationship we had which was built on trust and fun. What we found we had, neither of us had ever

experienced before. Before I knew it, time had flown and it was my 19th birthday. What would he have planned this time, I asked myself – knowing it would be hard for him to top what he had done already. Paul had wonderful taste and the celebrations began with a romantic card and lovely gifts. He always seemed to know just what I wanted which further convinced me that we were right for each other. We went out for lunch and I was told that we were going somewhere special in the evening. He had booked a table somewhere expensive and told me to wear something nice.

Another thing I loved about being with Paul was that he made me feel sexy and alive. I felt like a woman. A taxi picked us up and took us to Oliver's and as we went downstairs into the restaurant I saw a beautiful little table set for two with candles. The butterflies in my stomach were flipping, I wasn't used to this kind of treatment and I was unfamiliar with restaurant etiquette. But the excitement I felt made me realise that I loved the life I had. The meal was gorgeous and Paul was endeared with me because I hadn't had many experiences like it. I didn't understand everything on the menu – and what were all the knives and forks on either side all about? Paul reassured me and loved

the fact that I was so excited about the evening, the ambiance, the meal and the "grown-up" thing.

We ordered a bottle of white wine and I chose a fillet steak. Perhaps not that adventurous but you have to remember I was learning! We ate, we drank and we talked about everything and anything as we gazed into each others' eyes. I was literally melting with happiness. We decided to walk home when we left the restaurant as we didn't have far to go. It was lovely holding hands as we walked along and I was grateful to get some air and some exercise. I had prepared myself for a night of birthday passion, but suddenly Paul seemed strained as we walked through the front door. "I've got a few bits to do upstairs then I'm off to bed," he said. "If you want to stay down and watch TV then I'll see you when you come up" he continued.

"But," I began before I stopped myself and decided not to ruin the evening with a childish outburst. Deep down I was pissed off. How could we go out and have a wonderful evening and then come to this? What had I done? Was he mad with me over something? I even wondered whether I'd eaten too much garlic and he

wanted to maintain a safe distance from me. I didn't know the answer and I didn't want to confront him either. I decided to let him be and I sat on the sofa brimming with anger. "Happy Birthday!" I muttered under my breath. After about 30 minutes Paul remained upstairs so I decided, still feeling in a huff, to join him. Just then I heard a noise coming from above me.

"Leanne" he said as he popped his head over the banisters looking down at me cheekily. "I found another birthday card up here for you". And, with that he threw the card down to me and disappeared once again. I sat on the stairs and wondered who the card could be from. Paul had already given me a beautiful card so I doubted that it was from him. As I pulled the card from the silver envelope I caught sight of the words: "Happy Birthday to my Darling Fiancée". There was a lovely picture of a couple dancing and I sat there and wondered if it was a joke. Had he picked the wrong card by mistake? Inside, Paul had written that he knew I liked surprises but before I could finish reading he called out: "Are you coming up then?" All of a sudden I felt really shy. I felt nervous about going upstairs. What if I'd read the card incorrectly? Then

again, what if it wasn't wrong, did he really mean this?

As I walked slowly upstairs I was conscious that my heart was beating faster than ever and I noticed our bedroom door was closed. I gasped as I opened the door; there, kneeling on one knee was Paul holding out a box with a stunning solitaire ring. I couldn't look. I, for once, was speechless. "Will you marry me Leanne?" he asked. He was still on the floor and the next few minutes were hazy as he pulled me towards him and placed the sparkler on my finger on my left hand. For those of you wondering, I said: "Yes", immediately. We lay in each others' arms and eventually I put my arms across my chest and smiled as I looked at my new ring before I drifted off to sleep.

The following morning I was up early. It felt just like Christmas and I wanted to make sure I hadn't been dreaming. Sure enough, there it was still firmly on my finger. I got ready quickly before Paul woke up as I wanted to look at my most glamorous before he saw me. Before he saw his fiancée. Even thinking about the word fiancée made me feel more alive. So there I was, looking glamorous and ready to face the world with our news. I didn't want to make the round of usual phone calls – I

wanted to tell everyone in person. As soon as Paul was ready we made the journey to Feock to give the good news to Trina and Peter and then raced to see my parents. I felt nervous, embarrassed and shy. As we met mum inside the house I felt as if I was going to burst with excitement. But, I was desperate to hide the surprise and so I'd covered my hands with a pair of gloves. We had planned to drag it out, but I'm not good at keeping things to myself for long and when we were talking about the birthday evening the night before I told them what presents Paul had given me. "Oh…and there was one other thing", I said as I whipped off the gloves. I was beaming.

Well, my mum started screaming and everyone was hugging and later, while dad and Paul had that "man-to-man" chat, mum and I gossiped in the kitchen. She mentioned about ideas for wedding themes and outfits, but I explained that I was still young and that we wanted to have fun and take our time. We weren't planning on getting married the following day. We followed up our news with a fantastic engagement party. Both sets of parents announced the news in the local paper and it was a special time.

JUST A *Step*

I'd joined a netball team encouraged by my Auntie Tina who was sporty like me and I was looking forward to the adrenaline buzz once again. Paul is a massive sports fan – hockey in winter, cricket in the summer with football, tennis and badminton in between. It was the perfect time for me to get off my backside and get training again. When I put on the netball bib for the first time in a while my pulse was racing and it felt great to be competitive once more. I reasoned I had a little way to go before I was completely fit again – I wasn't 15 years old anymore.

Chapter 3

Sorrow of my heart

Okay, so here goes with the start of the "nitty gritty" in my life. This is the chapter that I have dreaded writing because it is the one closest to my heart and will reveal how my story unfolds.

I noticed one day that my big toe and the toe next to it were rather swollen on my left foot. It was almost as if the toes had fused together, but I didn't worry too much and put it down to just being something and nothing in the same way I would have done if I'd suddenly developed a bunion or got a verucca. I'd damaged my ankle during gymnastics at school a couple of years before and wondered if it might have had anything to do with that. Otherwise, I didn't let it bother me too much. Over a few days I noticed that the movement in my toes was feeling slightly restricted, but still I didn't worry.

You think when you're young that you're

indestructible. I certainly believed that that was the case with me. I was working hard to build my career and I lived with the man of my dreams. Although there were ups and downs, life was otherwise happy and normal and I found I was immensely contented. One wintry weekend in October 2002, Paul managed to get four tickets for my parents and us to go and see Robbie Williams in concert. Paul and I had often been out with my parents – after all Paul was similar in age to mum and dad and we enjoyed spending time together. I was looking forward to going but when the time came, I found I didn't feel particularly well. I felt extremely tired and had a headache that was making me feel sick. I was generally unwell so I decided that I was better off at home and waved the three of them off – telling them to have a great time – as they left without me. Although I'm comfortable in my own company, I invited Donna over for the weekend and I enjoyed planning some of the things we could do together; girly movies, popcorn, a takeaway – *Sex In The City* – eat your heart out.

The evening turned out to be great as we plied ourselves with chocolate and had a good gossip about old

school friends; who was pregnant or who was engaged. After a while, I went upstairs to take out some bedding from the airing cupboard for Donna but as I reached for the spare supply of pillows my ankle suddenly gave way beneath me. The next thing I knew, I was on the floor screaming in agony. What had happened? Had I blacked out or fainted? Lots of questions were racing through my mind but the overwhelming one that kept coming up was, "What could I do about the pain racing down my leg?"

Donna came running up the stairs having heard me cry out and I tried to choke back the tears and look brave without much success. I've always been a bit of a baby when it comes to pain. We both thought it was probably a sprained ankle, but the pain got progressively worse as the evening wore on and we decided that a trip to casualty was in order. I managed to stumble my way to the car and Donna drove me to the local hospital. I wasn't worried, after all, it couldn't be anything serious as I'd probably just fallen over and my ankle had given way.

I soon regretted the decision to go to hospital as the hours passed by. We were still sitting in the waiting room at two o'clock in the morning. Maybe it's a clever tactic

they try – the longer you wait the more annoyed you feel and the less likely you are to remember what you went there for in the first place? After some moaning and a great deal of yawning I was eventually taken to see the doctor. "Yes, Leanne…probably a sprained ankle," he mumbled. His response was no surprise and I was beginning to feel extremely guilty about having dragged my friend along to hear that it was probably just a sprain. I thought she might think I was pathetic. However, he said: "We'll send you for an X-ray, just to be on the safe side." "What? Another hour?" I asked myself. But, I was quickly wheeled into X-ray and after a few quick "blasts" from the machine I was back in front of the doctor. He was now looking intently at the pictures of my ankle. "Mmm," he said as he seemed to be thoroughly examining the stills. "I'm going to send you for another scan." "Nothing to worry about Leanne," he added, "It's just that I can see a little shadow on your X-rays and I want to double check that it's nothing."

"Okay, thank you" I replied. I was just simply relieved that at last I could go home. Armed with a tubi-grip, crutches and a box which seemed laden with medicine,

Donna and I finally made it home again.

The whole thing didn't really worry me, however naïve that may sound. The pain slowly subsided after taking some pills and I managed to get a good night's sleep that was worry free from my point of view. You hear about how long it takes to get an appointment with the trusty NHS so I was a little surprised to receive a date for my scan after only a couple of days following my night in casualty. The letter said that I would be having an MRI scan. As this was something I knew very little about I was neither scared nor worried by the prospect. I booked the day off work and the night before I carefully read through the instructions in the letter so that I understood everything I needed to do in preparation.

When the day of the appointment arrived I dressed myself in baggy clothes as instructed and chose a CD to play while the scan took place. The thing that upset me most was that I wasn't allowed to wear any make-up. Scary! Paul had also booked the day off work and as he drove me to hospital I found to my surprise that I grew increasingly nervous. Paul tried to make small talk and lovingly put his hand on my knee, but I didn't want to speak. I smiled and

said I just wanted to concentrate on getting this thing over with so that I could get back home as soon as possible.

When we arrived, we headed for a small unit near the back of the hospital. We were told that only I could go into the building, so Paul went back to wait in the car. This worked out well for me as the fact that he was sat outside waiting made me feel that we could leave all the sooner. As I undressed to put on the gown provided, I saw a young lad come out from another room. It made me think about it. "Yes, this was probably just a sprain….it could even be a sports injury and what did that mean? Nothing! Possibly a few weeks off netball, maybe even some time to put my feet up." In my mind, it was certainly nothing serious.

I felt a little calmer as I went into the next room – it was just like I'd seen on the television – it was small with a "tunnel" in the centre. The nurses tried reassuring me but as I got up on the bed the nerves started to kick in. They got worse as the bed and I started slowly moving nearer and nearer the "tunnel". I tried to breathe deeply and told myself that "it was nothing. It would be over shortly, and, yes, it wasn't going to be pleasant, but I was a big girl now and I'd get through it." I mean, how bad could it be?

I closed my eyes as everyone left the room. They had given me some headphones so that I could listen to my chosen CD. The staff were also able to talk to me through an earpiece and they told me to lay very still. Isn't it strange how when you are told not to do something you feel an overwhelming urge to do it? My breathing suddenly went crazy as I began to panic. I didn't like being in the tunnel – it felt claustrophobic and scary. "Concentrate Leanne," I told myself. "The more still you stay, the quicker it's over." The music stopped and the lady next door suddenly yelled in my ear: "Leanne, you must stay still." This was making it worse, not better. Not only was I making the whole process longer, now I was annoying the staff!

An hour had passed and we still weren't finished and what was supposed to be a simple scan had turned into a living nightmare. I opened my eyes and stared hard at the ceiling. My attention was focused on TRYING NOT TO MOVE.

At that moment, I thought my pain and suffering was over as the door opened and two nurses raced in. I went to get up and felt a beam spread across my face as the two

women I thought of as angels at that moment appeared. But my relief was short-lived and my face quickly changed as I saw the look on theirs. They were concerned. "Leanne, we really need you to stay still…the more you move the longer it's going to take and we need to take a closer look at something," said one. "Oh, okay," I whimpered as the hell continued. I lay there determined and continued to stare at the ceiling. Eventually I started to drift off to sleep. The next thing I was aware of was the nurses being back in the room. They had hold of my left arm and one of them was holding a needle. "I don't understand," I pleaded, "What's happening? What's wrong? I'm scared of needles, please tell me what's happening. Please, I'm frightened." "We've found something Leanne and we've called the doctor over," was their answer. "He shouldn't be long."

The words washed over me not really sinking in. Was something seriously wrong with me? The needles had injected a fluid into my body to enable them to look deeper and get a clearer picture of what might be wrong. My arm was rested across my chest and once again, I was told to keep still. The nurses left the room and the bed slowly moved back inside the "tunnel". The tears were

rolling down my face and I felt paralysed. I couldn't sob and I couldn't scream. I couldn't have a cuddle with my mum who would have told me it would all be okay. All I could do was stare at the ceiling as tears of sadness and fear continued to roll down my cheeks.

My misery was interrupted as the door opened yet again and the staff pulled me out of the "tunnel". "We've found a tumour," I was told bluntly. "You will be contacted by the hospital to discuss it further. You may get dressed now." Had they *actually* just said those words to me, I thought. Had they *just* said the word TUMOUR? I felt sick and weak. Did they just tell me I had cancer? I felt confused by the emotional mixture of what they had told me, the trauma of what I had just been through and the overwhelming relief that the scan was finally over. I had a sip of water and just wanted to get out of the hospital mobile unit. Paul was sitting outside in the car. I had never seen such a welcoming sight and no matter what might happen in the future, following the results, I was finally free of that machine.

I got in the car and for once I was silent. Paul, understanding as ever, didn't press me to speak and he

just placed his hand on my thigh and stroked it. We set off and drove in silence for a few minutes before he asked me what I wanted to do. "I want to see my mum," I replied. What is it about needing your mum when things are tough? Paul knew that that was where I wanted to go and I think he thought it would probably help me too. Paul, who is close to my parents, understands how much I love them and one of his greatest strengths is his unconditional support. We pulled up outside where my mum was working. She came to the entrance and ran out towards me. She hugged me so tight that I instantly felt safe. "What did they say?" she asked quietly. My tear-stained face was a give-away and said a million things I was literally unable to say for myself. "They found a tumour…" I stuttered. That was all I could say as mum, Paul and I all hugged each other.

We spent that evening with my parents and Chris. A sort of family crisis meeting you might say – although not much was said. There was a reassuring "It'll be fine" from my dad and "Don't worry about anything, sis" from my brother. There were teary smiles from my mum and the ever prominent touch from Paul. But, deep down, I didn't

think that anyone was convinced and we were all just as scared no matter what we did or didn't say that night. After a few days had passed I began to feel quite positive. "I'm young," I thought, "I can't die at my age, I still have so much more to do." I went back to work and decided to tell everyone. I didn't want sympathy, but I wanted my friends and colleagues to know and the "If there's anything I can do" choccies never did any harm! Then it happened – the phone call to say that a biopsy had been booked – which was followed by a letter telling me what to bring into hospital. As I looked at the date for the biopsy, I realised that my parents, Chris and his then girlfriend were all booked to go on holiday the day after the appointment.

"We'll cancel it," my parents offered as soon as they found out. "There's no way we're going away." I knew this would be their reaction so I was prepared with my response. "I promise you," I said, "I will be fine. It's only a biopsy and I won't be too poorly afterwards. And, anyway, I want you to go. I would feel sad if you didn't, please go…it will make me happy." Maybe I played the sympathy card on that occasion as I really did want them to go on their holiday. The thought of seeing them all

upset around me was unbearable, so after a great deal of persuasion, they agreed that they would go. Getting through the biopsy and then my family going off for a break was a warming thought and I did want them to have a break from the world of tumours and fear that I had suddenly thrown them into.

On the day of the biopsy, I was busy packing for hospital while my family were busy packing for their holiday. Even though we were all busy, we all had one thing on our minds. Mum and I went to Asda that morning to buy some essentials for my hospital stay. I think it was really an excuse for us to spend some time together. "Everything will be okay my darling," she said. "I know mummy, I'll be fine, promise," I replied. Mum, dad, Paul and I all made the trip to the hospital and I was upbeat when asking them what plans they had for their trip. I didn't want to concentrate on what would be happening later that day. I wanted to talk about fun things and things that I planned to do when this was all over.

When we entered the hospital, Paul carried my overnight bag and we wandered down the corridor to the

ward I'd be staying on. As we got closer, I could see my consultant standing by the door. He was dressed in a suit which I thought was unusual and he shook our hands in turn before asking us to join him in a side room. Was this usual procedure? We all sat down and then the consultant explained that he had had a good look at all the scans. He was slightly concerned and that when the biopsy was carried out, some tissue that was to be removed might be taken by courier to Newcastle for specialists to take a look at it. Afterwards a nurse showed me to my bed and after a couple of hours I was told I needed to get ready. I undressed in the toilet and came out to be met by the loving faces of my family. I know I must have looked awful – I mean, no make-up and no hairspray! Not only that, my bum was hanging out of the dowdy hospital gown. I tried really hard to put on a brave face and told everyone that I'd soon be okay. I said I felt fine but my false smile soon faded when two porters arrived to take me to theatre.

My teeth started chattering and I couldn't stop shaking. I was suddenly petrified. Before we took the final turn to the theatre, we stopped briefly so I could kiss Paul and my dad who was stroking my head. They both told

JUST A *Step*

me they loved me. Mum was allowed into the anaesthetic room with me and I think we were living off each other's nerves while my plan to be brave for everyone had failed. I felt I was making it worse. Mum had to wear a gown and once she had changed, she held my hand all the way to the theatre and into the little room where the surgeons were waiting. "I love you my darling...I'll be here when you wake up," she sobbed as she kissed me. I counted to ten as instructed. "One, two..." I was gone.

"It's all over Leanne – you're fine," a kind nurse told me as I came to, drowsy and unaware of my surroundings. The first thing I felt was relief. I had got through it and I was alive. It was an amazing feeling. Still under the effects of the anaesthetic I fought quickly to get better. One of the benefits of being young is that you tend to "bounce back" more quickly and before I knew it I was being wheeled back to the ward and even the oxygen mask covering my face couldn't keep me from smiling as I faced my family. My mum sat and stroked my head as I dozed in and out of sleep over the next few hours. You have probably worked out by now that I love being stroked and I sometimes wonder if I was a cat in a previous life!

By the evening I was off the oxygen and sitting up chatting as usual. I even used the payphone to call granny, gran and gramps to let them know I was okay. They had been worried and I just wanted to put their minds at rest. I was excited that Chris would soon be coming to see me when he finished work and I felt a sense of pride that I had got through it. The atmosphere was much lighter than it had been and it was obvious that we all felt a huge sense of relief. Mum and dad started talking about their well-deserved holiday and it was great to talk about something other than me. I loved the feeling when I lay back on the bed and closed my eyes. I could just listen to them talking. When it was dark outside someone came and turned on the light beside my bed. Then the surgeon entered and I could tell instantly that he was anxious. The tall, strong man who was dressed smartly and had an authoritative air about him suddenly looked nervous. He scratched his head and then said: "Could I have a quick word with mum and dad?"

It was fine by me and I assumed he just wanted to tell them how the operation went and how long it would take for me to get my full strength back. Paul stayed with me as

JUST A *Step*

I lay there waiting for my brother to arrive. An hour must have passed and my parents were still not back. Panic started to creep in and I said: "Do you think everything's okay, Paul?" "Of course, darling...everything will be fine. Don't worry." I have always been able to rely on Paul to make me feel better and it helped reassure me that there was nothing to worry about.

Our chat was interrupted by a nurse who came over and started to pull the curtains around my bed. "We've sent your parents outside to get some fresh air," she offered helpfully. "They won't be long now." "Fresh air – why would they need fresh air?" I asked myself. "What on earth had they been told?" Paul held my hand. When dad came back onto the ward he was alone. He sat by me and put his hand on my lap. "Mum will be here in a minute," he said, "She's fine." But *he* didn't look fine and I didn't believe a word he was saying. "Is everything okay, dad?" I asked nervously. "Everything is okay," he replied. Dad would never lie to me so I asked him again. "Do you promise, dad?" With that, he started to cry. I had never seen my dad cry before and it shook me to the core. My mum returned as my dad sat in tears and she was trying to

hide the fact that she too had been sobbing. Chris was with my mum. My dad tried really hard to find the words to explain.

"When they opened your foot, they expected to find it pink and fleshy, but it was hard and black." He tried to continue: "The surgeons opened it up and just looked at each other as they all knew it was bad news." He didn't need to say anything else – I understood full well what was going on. Trying to be practical I said: "So, what are they going to do about it?" I wanted to know what exactly could be done to solve it. Mum then stepped forward and while choking back her tears she explained that: "The part of you that has this, might have to be taken away." And, with that, we were all silent, apart from the sound of my mum sobbing quietly.

Nothing needed to be said and that was how we stayed for the next hour as I lay back on the bed, closed my eyes and just told them that: "I'll be okay. Don't worry." I also said I would cope. I didn't shed one tear and I found it more important to hold it together for everyone. I had never forgotten what my mum had once said: "When you are smiling, I am smiling," and it's like a rule that I've

always tried to live by. I knew that if I broke down it would just make things worse for all of us. "You guys can go," I said as I sat up a while later. I felt more alert and had even started tucking into the bucket of Maltesers that Chris had brought me.

With a pile of magazines to look through, I told my family that I'd be fine and that they should go home and get some rest. After all, it had also been an emotionally long day for them. They all hugged and kissed me in a way that let me know they all loved me. I also realised that they were all scared – and so was I. It is really strange, but once they left and I was alone, I suddenly realised what had happened. I lay there with my thoughts and I felt scared. "What did the future hold? Would I really lose a part of my leg? Would my life change forever? Who knew?" But, one thing I did know was that I wasn't going to waste my energy worrying. I would tackle it head on and make it as painless as I could, not just for me, but for the four people that had just left me. The people I loved.

The following morning, both my parents and Paul came to collect me when I was allowed to go home and I couldn't wait. Mum and dad had decided not to go on

holiday and I knew that however much I protested that arguments weren't going to work. Instead they had booked a last minute holiday for the four of us at Butlins in Minehead. The nurses said goodbye and told me they'd be in touch again shortly. The plan was to go back into hospital in a few weeks time where they would perform the "big" operation of removing the tumour. One nurse also told me that the extent of the tumour was unknown and they wouldn't know how large it was until they operated. I was told to forget all about it – easier said than done – go on holiday and enjoy myself. Butlins was great and I threw myself into every activity going, although obviously, I couldn't quite forget about what was looming and at the back of my mind the thought of what was going to happen when I returned home was very real.

Once I was back home, I prepared myself in every way that I could. My employers were very understanding and proved themselves once again to be unconditionally supportive. Knowing that I had so many people wishing me well and spurring me on made me feel stronger. Then, like a speeding bullet, D-Day arrived. We made yet another silent journey to the hospital and it seemed as if

my life was on replay as we entered the ward for the second time and I got settled in. This time, as I went to the toilets to change into the ghastly hospital gown that strangled my neck and bared my bum, I looked in the mirror and saw the make-up free face and straight loose hair. I looked like a patient – I felt vulnerable – and there, alone in the loos, I felt scared. I didn't want to make this any worse on my family than it had to be so after a moment alone, I gathered myself together and went out fronting a false smile. It was the same as the one they were all wearing!

As they handed me the pre-med, I lay, feeling small on my bed, waiting for the two porters that would come and take me down that lonely corridor. "Be brave, Leanne!" I told myself trying to coach my own mind into handling the situation with ease. But, frankly, it wasn't that easy. Then, there they were. I could swear I'd had nightmares about these two men. Taking me away – taking me somewhere frightening – taking me somewhere I couldn't guarantee I would come back from. Once again, it was a repeat performance when my teeth started to chatter, just as they had a few weeks before. Like the last time, both Paul and my dad kissed me and mum, dressed

in her obligatory gown, held my hand tightly. I can't tell you how long I was under the anaesthetic exactly, but one thing was for sure, when I woke this time I felt bad – really, really bad – I felt like I'd been in some horrendous accident and the pain was literally unbearable. "Was I still in theatre?" I questioned myself as the nurses tried to reassure me.

The relief hit me as I was reunited on the ward with my family, but instead of raising a smile under my oxygen mask, I simply lay on the bed, limp and in pain. I was struggling to breathe and the oxygen mask was to stay tightly over my face. I certainly wasn't "bouncing back" this time. The operation had taken its toll and the surgeon explained that they had cut from my toe to my ankle on the top of my foot and then repeated it underneath my foot so that they could peel back the skin on both sides. The tumour that had turned my foot hard and black was neatly nestling inside me and proved to be the size of a tennis ball. "Who would have thought something that large could have grown so quickly inside me – and why had I been totally unaware of it?" The surgeon described the tumour taking over inside my foot like ivy growing into

every open space available. It had made the surgery difficult and it had taken the stuffing – quite literally – out of me.

A few days passed and I slowly, after much rest, loads of oxygen and a number of drugs, began to regain some strength although I still felt desperately ill. I also felt overwhelmingly sick and it was taking everything I had to get over the operation. Just as I started to feel as if I might be on some sort of road to recovery and reclaim back some of my own spirit, the consultant arrived to explain that next on the agenda was six weeks of intense radiotherapy which would take place for five days each week. Call me stupid, but I didn't really understand anything about radiotherapy. "Would I lose my hair? Would I be constantly sick?" I just didn't know and as someone pushed me in a wheelchair to the oncology department I once again felt quite petrified. Oncology was situated in the basement of the hospital and there was something scary about it. The lift on the way down seemed dark and it began to make me feel worse about the whole ordeal. But, although what was going to happen wasn't the best experience in the world, the reassuring smiles and the

kind words from the staff helped a great deal.

I looked around the room and quickly discovered that I was the youngest patient by far. The saddest thing that struck me was not the fact that I was there too, but that many poorly people were there, like me, having treatment. There were elderly couples holding hands, so obviously in love and so obviously scared of losing one another. There was a lady in a headscarf in the corner reading a magazine and there were a number of people lying on beds – too ill to sit up. "Could I cope seeing this every day?" It was a moving situation that made me forget my own troubles for a time and I felt that I didn't belong in that room. "Surely I wasn't as poorly as these people?" I felt like a bit of a fraud sitting there in the wheelchair. I was young and determined and I wanted to get better as soon as possible so that I could get back out onto a netball court or drive my car somewhere – anywhere! I was moved from the waiting area to a white room with a massive machine in the centre. It looked like something out of the movies and okay, looking back, I might possibly have been feeling like a bit of a drama queen, but at the time everything seemed magnified and I was once again being thrown into a world

that I was both scared and unsure of.

A lovely lady, called Pat, put her arm around me and explained what would happen during my treatment. She then helped me onto the daunting machine and began to unwrap my bandages. It was only the second time since the operation that I had seen my foot and it wasn't looking pretty. It looked concave and it was obvious that something had been "scooped" out. My foot was covered in so many wiry black stitches that they seemed to cover it completely. It looked like every piece of possible skin had a stitch in it. Isn't it strange that when you look at something out of the ordinary and gory that it feels much more painful? I decided not to look at it anymore. Yes, I was still in my gown – and as I lay there two small "tattoos" were injected onto my foot so that they could direct the radiation in the same place each time. This would give the treatment a greater chance of working and would ensure that it could kill off any nasty cells that thought they could lurk undetected.

I had the room to myself while the treatment was carried out and it made me feel lonely and scared. The tears began to run down my face. "Could I really put up

with this every day for six weeks?" Hang on, reality check. The treatment wasn't painful, but the whole situation had been an emotional rollercoaster for some time now. I had tried to be brave in front of everyone I knew as I wanted them to feel better than I knew they did. But, having treatment was somewhere I could go alone and could allow myself to have my *own* feelings about what was happening to me. It was somewhere I could take off my "mask" and for five days a week, for six weeks, I was able to be myself – scared, vulnerable and afraid.

Chapter 4

Goodbye for today

Six weeks seemed like a lifetime, but I stuck to the treatment plan and told myself that whatever happened next, the treatment and I had given it our best shot.

But, it wasn't just emotional scars that I suffered during treatment. The "light sunburn" effects that were described in the helpful radiotherapy leaflet eventually looked more like third degree burns. My left foot was raw and covered in a painful rash that also made my skin "weep" and it leaked profusely. The physiotherapist had fitted me with an odd looking type of "ski boot" – which later became cool when David Beckham was given one! However, needless to say, my NHS version wasn't so flashy and it really didn't go with the sexy high heel that I wanted to wear on my right foot. I also discovered that it didn't look that good with a feminine outfit either. Night time was worst. I was scratching desperately at my aggravated foot. To ease the itching I would drag my foot along the carpet or reach

down with a hairbrush to ease it. The only thing I couldn't do was use my fingernails. The thought of my fingers and nails passing over the prominent scars that were so very sensitive just made me feel physically sick. Sometimes the itch would be so bad that I would spend literally hours in the bath which seemed to ease it. But the relief was short-lived once I got out of the water and I can honestly say that the itch was far worse than the pain – at least I could ease that with drugs. As well as the constant unforgiving irritation, my foot no longer resembled what it once was. It became a burden and was so weak that I found myself constantly resorting to wearing the "fashionable" ski boot.

Having the foot contraption tied to me 24 hours a day, seven days a week did get me down but, as I had always done so far, I coped and put on my mask to make everyone think I was doing okay. I went away for a weekend with friends. Okay, I wasn't a whiz on the dance floor, but I did have fun and tried to feel young once again. I also tried to put the trauma of the previous months behind me for a little while. When I got back home I was quickly back into the swing of my job and it gave me some normality and structure. I thrived being at work and looking back, I think

it gave me a kind of escape. I never found going to work a chore and I was lucky. As well as being financially independent and paying the bills, I had a great big extended family to see every day. I had been working for Carrick almost since I left school and although I had begun as a trainee in the legal department, and obviously, hadn't been to university, I was given the chance to go to college on a part-time basis so I could gain further qualifications.

I was aware that a university education wasn't everything. My mum was a shining example of that. She had left school with few qualifications, but had never been short of job offers because of her personality, hard work and determination. She was my inspiration and had always told me to make myself like a sponge. "Take in everything," she said, "and learn from every experience you have." I worked hard and learned new skills along the way so that within a few months I had been offered a promotion. That made me feel proud and even though my colleagues knew I was ill and wouldn't be the fastest worker to make it to the post room they believed in me and that boosted my confidence no end.

LEANNE GROSE

At last, everything was going well again – work, my relationship with Paul and basically life in general. The only issue at the time was the bloody boot! But then, I was hit with something else. A letter in the post from the hospital asked me to see another surgeon for a review. At the time, I felt like I was on the "run" – excuse the pun – from the Hospital Police. I didn't want to "go back inside", but they had caught up with me. So, back Paul and I went once again to the hospital. I asked him to wait for me outside as I had always found it easier to go in on my own. I wanted to deal with whatever they had to say to me next so that I could relay what I wanted to in my own way later on. I wanted to soften the blow. I walked in feeling quite confident – after all – what more could they do to me now? I was introduced to the new surgeon and I was asked to go and lie on the bed. The ever-faithful boot was removed and he looked intently at my sore foot which by now, while still bearing the ever-itchy rash, had turned hard and shiny. I almost didn't recognise my own foot and as the surgeon ran his fingers over it I couldn't feel a thing. It was numb. Although it still itched like crazy, there were no other feelings there at all. "Okay, Leanne...please come

and take a seat." I tried – as is my way – to crack some jokes to lighten the mood, but they fell on deaf ears as he looked at the floor with a deadly serious expression. Perhaps he thought I wasn't taking the consultation seriously, or that's certainly the impression he gave when he said in a serious voice: "Leanne, we are going to have to amputate your foot." I hadn't been trying to be funny and I hadn't wanted to have a party during the consultation, joking was my coping mechanism.

"Umm, no…no…thank you," I said as I shook his hand and headed for the door. I felt the situation was strange. I wanted to make what he was telling me easier for him so I flashed him my "I'm absolutely fine" smile and left the room. As I walked towards Paul who was waiting in the car for me I mentally prepared how I was going to deal with the situation. I started: "Before you say anything Paul, I want you to know that I am absolutely fine…I really am…but they are going to remove my foot." There, I'd said it. I looked at him and he looked away and was silent. "Honestly Paul," I ventured, "I'm going to be fine." In fact, the more I said it, the more I believed it. What did this foot mean to me now anyway? Pain and discomfort. And, maybe this was what I

needed to move on in my life – it certainly didn't seem to be getting any better.

I can't say it was easy telling everyone, but I didn't want anyone to hear on the "grapevine" either so I made the effort to visit all my family and friends to tell them myself. I wanted them to see that *I* was okay with the idea and sometimes I felt as if I was coaching them through it to make it as easy for them as possible. You'd never have thought it was me who would be having the operation! Over the next few weeks I made a lot of preparations. I like to plan and at that moment in time, things felt so uncertain that I wanted everything to run as smoothly as it possibly could. I put in extra hours at the office to ensure that all my work was up to date and most evenings I went to see people I cared about. I especially spent a lot of time with my granny who was desperately worried about me. I knew that she would have rather been the one going through it, not me, and I tried to reassure her I was fine and could cope. She was unwell herself and, at the time, I didn't want to add to her worries or make her feel worse.

Despite my resolve to stay strong and calm, especially in front of all those around me, I found myself feeling low

one evening as I asked myself "What the hell is going to happen to me? Will I come out of this alive?" I know it sounds completely absurd, but I couldn't, at the time, understand how someone could actually survive this sort of operation. I mean, how can they physically remove part of your body without you bleeding to death? This thought had actually been on my mind for quite some time and I had spent nights thinking and worrying about it and basically it kept coming back to the fact that I feared the worst. I didn't actually think I would live.

Paul had gone out for the evening. I felt really down and I was alone. I went into the study and decided to sit at the computer and write letters to my family just in case all my worst fears came true. "Just in case," I told myself. I even started writing a list of songs that I would want played at my funeral. Call me morbid, but at the time it seemed strangely therapeutic and it felt like an opportunity to tell everyone how I was really feeling. The song list was the easy part; Bon Jovi's "Thank You For Loving Me" encapsulated everything I would want to say and then I chose "The Rose" by Bette Midler. There were several reasons for this second choice. Not only was it a beautiful song which this woman

performed with amazing power, but I had recently found out that Chris had listened to it a lot when I first became ill. Because it was special to him, it was special to me. I turned to the letters. This was not so easy and, for someone would could have won awards for talking, I was suddenly lost for words, I mean, how could I tell people that meant the world to me how I felt about them? I nearly didn't continue.

Tears rolled down my face as I nervously typed the words.

My darling mummy
 This really is the hardest thing I have ever typed in my life and if you are reading this it means I have gone. But, believe me, I am always with you. You made me and I'll always be your daughter.

I stopped.

What if I left mum's letter until last? Each letter I wrote basically ripped me in two, but there was just something about that letter to my mum…

I told my dad how proud I was to be his daughter, and that I had had an amazing life. I put that down to two

fabulous parents. I thanked him for always being there for me and for looking after us all. I told him that I desperately loved him and always would. I also said that I knew how much he loved all of us and I also asked him to look after Paul. I knew sitting there writing it that the letter would be unbearable for him to read but I knew that he would do all that I asked of him and I wanted Paul to remain a part of my family.

I told the brother I adore that he had made my life fun and that I had had a fantastic childhood growing up with him. I said I'd always be his big sister and that I was proud of him. I urged him to go for everything in life and to achieve things for the two of us.

In Paul's letter, I thanked him for looking after me through all the ups and downs and I told him that I was so blessed to have met him. I also said that I didn't regret a second of the time we had spent together. I didn't want him to be lonely in life so I wrote that I wanted him to find happiness again with someone else – although I did give strict instructions that she wasn't to be too pretty or too slim! I finished the letter with the words that I would love him for always. When it came to my granny I wrote that I

would always be okay and I told her how much she meant to me and that I loved her so much. I told her how amazing she was and that she had kept me laughing and smiling.

When I returned to the letter to my mum, I finished with the words that I wanted to thank her for being my best friend and that I loved her so deeply. That would never die.

Writing the letters made me feel so selfish. I mean, how could I do this to them? How could I leave? How could life go on without me? I saved the letters on the computer and wiped my tears. I think writing the letters that night made me realise for the first time exactly what a big deal it all was and that things might just hang in the balance.

It wasn't long before my mask was firmly back on and I continued with my preparations for the operation. I said goodbye to work colleagues and friends and when it came to actually leaving, I hugged them all tightly. I didn't want to let anyone go.

The 11th day of the 11th month at 11.00am. Now, was that a good omen, or a bad one? Isn't it weird how you

analyse everything when you are scared. I didn't want the entire family to troop into the hospital with me so Paul and I went together. For some reason, the fewer of us there were, the less of a deal it actually seemed to be. We went to the ward quietly and I settled in for the third time. But settling in this time wasn't as easy as I was horrified that I had been given a room to myself.

I realise that some people would find this easier, and it would have been perfect, however, I didn't want to be alone and shut away from the world. I wanted people around so that I could be distracted and so after persuading the ward staff that I would be better elsewhere, the following day I was moved onto a shared ward. And that's where I met Marjorie, a little lady in her seventies, with whom I clicked immediately. Her spirit was more like that of a teenager than an elderly woman and we quickly made friends. When we were both told that we would be having our legs removed on the same day we formed an instant bond. She became my salvation and she made me laugh. We giggled constantly and were akin to two naughty teenagers. I was admitted to hospital a week prior to the operation as, because I was so young, the hospital wanted

me to be fully prepared for what would be happening. The week's preparation was fine by me. I like to know what's happening and I like to feel prepared. But the preparations were quite sparse on the whole.

A counsellor visited me for a few minutes and decided that I was well aware of what was happening to me and that basically I'd already prepared myself. Physiotherapists had also been to visit and had explained the basic exercises that I would need to do after the operation. Also, because I was there for some days before my own surgery, I had been exposed to other patients on the ward leaving to have their own amputations. When they returned to the ward and they'd obviously survived, it did help me mentally to prepare myself for what was to come.

The week went frighteningly quickly although there were moments when I actually forgot why exactly I was there. There were some lighter moments that took my mind off what would be happening in few days time plus I began to believe that, "yes, I will survive this." My family visited every day, although my granny still wasn't well enough to come in and see me. I knew how desperately she wanted to visit, but I knew she was better off staying at

home, so I would sit in the day room and talk to her from the pay phone. Maybe that's another reason why I felt so close to Marjorie that week – she reminded me of granny and it was comforting to be around her. The day before my operation everything was prepared and I received a lovely surprise.

"Leanne, you have the afternoon off," I was told. This was music to my ears. I was allowed to leave the hospital but I had strict instructions that I wasn't to be "Too late back," they said. My mum came to pick me up and I felt free. At the time, although it felt good to be getting out for a few hours I think I was in total denial at what would be happening to me the following day. I almost felt, leaving that afternoon that I was getting out of the whole situation, finally. We sat in the car and mum asked me where I wanted to go? Shopping? To the beach? I could go wherever I wanted. "Please take me to see granny," I said. We didn't ring to warn her we were coming – I wanted to surprise her and when we arrived, mum let me go in first. I let myself into her house and walked quietly into her living room where granny was sitting in her usual chair by the window. "Hey, granny," I said as I walked over and

flung my arms around her.

I was a little taken aback by the way she looked when I saw her. She seemed quieter than usual and a bit disorientated. It frightened me that this strong woman seemed slightly vulnerable and I knew she wasn't well. I hated seeing her like this. Throughout the afternoon she seemed to become more coherent and we discussed that my operation would soon be over and I would soon be home. Talking to her that afternoon reminded me of the many hours I had spent with the woman I adored. Mum was in the kitchen sorting out one or two things for granny who started rooting through her bag. She always had lots of different things in her bag – it was like a treasure trove with hankies, mint imperials, glasses. She eventually found her purse and started to pass all her loose change to me. "Call me, darling," she said, "when it's all over." "I'll be fine, granny...I promise." I wanted to protect her from what was about to happen just as I did with the rest of my family. I wanted everyone to believe that I was absolutely okay about them taking away the lower part of my leg.

When it was time to go I remember hugging her for as long as possible and I smelled her hair. It smelt of

JUST A *Step*

talcum powder – it always did. I kissed her and as I was leaving she shouted: "I love you my darling." "I love you too granny," came my reply. Mum drove me back to the hospital.

Later that evening I was taken down to theatre to have an epidural. A huge needle was inserted into my spine so that I was numb from the waist downwards. But I wasn't alone and mum and Auntie Elaine were with me and both held my hands so tightly before I had been given the epidural on my way to theatre. I was feeling strong – and determined to show it – but I was also feeling incredibly sad. I knew that both mum and Elaine were worried about granny and it felt as if the world was, just for a moment, against my entire family. Despite the strength I had, it was an emotional moment and I started to cry. But, I wasn't just crying because of the things that were difficult, I was crying because I realised that my family were stuck together with a special kind of "glue" and nothing and nobody could rip us apart. Sleepily, following the epidural, I was wheeled back to the ward where I kissed my family goodbye and told them to get a good night's sleep. They all promised to be with me early in the morning.

I lay there with what seemed like a million thoughts running through my head and I was feeling pretty low. Then Marjorie called out to me across the ward and we talked and talked and talked late into the night. She helped me through what was such a difficult few hours and the help she gave me was priceless. When morning came the nurses came round to give us all a good wash. Knowing that I would be in my bed for a long time I was relieved that I was being spruced up. I wanted to feel clean. I lay quietly waiting for my family to arrive and I actually enjoyed having some final time alone. It had given me the opportunity to make a decision. "Do I sit and moan, feel sorry for myself and think the worst about being poorly?" No, I decided, "I get out there, stick that smile back on my face and I'll bloody well get better."

It brought a smile to my face when I decided that what I was actually going to do was tackle this situation head on. Maybe I wasn't the drama queen I'd always thought I was. Maybe I should give myself some credit. I was very young to have suffered a tumour and I was extremely young to be facing life without my leg. I looked down at my body. It was going to change and I closed my eyes and

lay back down on the bed as my head apologised to my body for letting it down.

Paul arrived first and my peace was interrupted. As always he looked calm, but I was slightly surprised that he had arrived first. It is a well-known fact that my family are always early – Paul, on the other hand is usually late. "Where's mum, dad and Chris?" I asked. "They're just running a bit late...they won't be long," came his reply. It did seem unusual, but then they arrived and there was no time to query it. Everyone was making the best of it for my sake. They were all there for me and I was there for them. Even though it was me going under the knife it may as well have been all of us – we were a team. All four of them kissed my leg goodbye. Yes, it sounds kind of strange, but it felt right at the time and perhaps it gave us all some kind of "closure". "They are ready for you Leanne," a nurse announced. I put the mask back on. I smiled. "Showtime."

There they were again, the two porters ready to take me to theatre. They wheeled my bed through the wards and as they pushed me towards the doors I slapped my hand with all the nurses in a "high five" salute as I went

past. I'd shouted "Good luck" to my friend Marjorie and me, being me, cracked jokes all the way...

We had a break with tradition and it was decided that this time, my dad would come into the anaesthetic room with me. Mum had agreed that her crying as I started my countdown might not be the best idea and Paul, although he tried hard not to, found the whole thing extremely difficult. I kissed all of them, silently praying that I would see all of them again as my dad held my hand on the way to theatre. They attached wires to my chest and I actually felt quite positive. It had been a challenge, it still was a challenge, but I was ready. I hated what had, and was, happening to me, but I had decided that the only way to move forward was to bite the bullet and get through it. My dad, dressed in a gown, held my hand as they injected the anaesthetic. "I love you daddy," I said. He remained silent. I realised he was choked and couldn't speak. "Well I hope you love me too?" I jested as the doctors laughed and my dad stroked my hair. He was stood behind my head and as I felt myself drifting I looked into his eyes. At that moment, I didn't want to see anyone else.

The hours past as my fretful family waited. I think that

the operation was harder for them – just waiting. At least I was asleep. I had no worries, but for them, conscious through every second of it, they had plenty. Then at last the news came, "Leanne's in recovery. She's okay and she will be fine." Meanwhile, as I lay in recovery, as before, the relief that it was finally over and that I was alive was overwhelming. The door to the recovery room opened and I struggled to turn my head. I was still dopey from the anaesthetic and I could feel pain but I was so pleased to see my mum and Chris enter the room. I remember that the first thing I did was to put my thumb up to my brother. It's still vivid in my mind and he knew then that I would be okay. After all, it was over. The next few hours were a haze as I slept on and off when they wheeled me back to the ward. I was connected to a lot of machines and the epidural in my back was giving me access to morphine which was regularly being pumped into my body to keep the pain stable.

It was a long day but by the evening I had started to come around more. The drugs that numbed me from the waist down had cut off all feelings to my legs and I didn't really feel as if my left leg was missing at all. They had

cleverly put a cage over the lower part of my body and covered it with a blanket. At least then you don't freak out when you wake up! I lay there feeling paralysed with my family around me. Paul and Chris left sometime later and my parents sat quietly with me. "It's over," I said, "I've done it." I felt quite proud of myself but I was still so drowsy that speaking was an effort. As my parents stood up to go, having told me to rest, I could clearly see something was wrong. "Mum?" I said as she looked at me with deeply sad eyes. "It's granny isn't it?"

"She's gone."

I just looked at my darling mum who had just suffered such loss and had had to sit with me following my amputation. "I love you mum. It'll be okay...we'll be okay." Dad kissed me and nothing more needed to be said. I lay there alone and I realised that my biggest loss that day wasn't my leg, it was granny. I would have sacrificed my other leg to have her back.

Even though losing her was the worst thing that had happened to me I felt surprisingly calm. Later that evening as I drifted in and out of sleep, feeling woozy and uncomfortable, I felt her presence at the end of my bed.

She was with me and I felt incredibly strong.

"Arghhhh!" I screamed as morning arrived. The pain had gradually been getting worse and it had now become unbearable. I felt like total crap and it felt like I'd been hit by a bus and run over – several times! Was it supposed to be this painful? Despite feeling terrible I found myself laughing when one of the nurses approached me and said: "Okay, Leanne, time to wash your undercarriage." But I wasn't particularly keen on having my "undercarriage" washed at that particular moment. I wanted to lie festering and I wanted to be left on my own, not pulled around. Mum was in early. She would make an amazing nurse and something about her made me feel better – but then, it always had. She was off work for a week having lost her mum and with me in hospital. I was relieved she was with me although neither of us mentioned granny much. It was too hard for us both.

Four ward staff then charged towards my bed and I knew that it was time to be prodded and poked. They had a washing up bowl and a warm towel and it was nice having my arms washed. It was good to feel refreshed but my feelings soon changed when they needed to move me. I

hadn't seen my legs since the operation and I was surprised that I still didn't want to. Not yet. I just wasn't ready. The four of them slid their hands underneath me and counted: "One, two, three, GO!" I cannot put into words how much it hurt. The pain was unbearable. It was as if a hot liquid – maybe blood – ran from one side of my leg to the other. I was sweating and shaking and screaming by this time and mum held my hand in support. I was in agony. Because the pain was ripping through me they washed me as quickly as they could and lay me back down. The experience was traumatic and I felt as if I'd never be able to move again. Even the little that I'd just had done had exhausted me and the nurses, knowing that granny had died the night before, kindly left mum and I alone and in peace.

She sat beside me and I felt helpless. I should have been able to hold her. She'd lost her mum and here she was, being strong for me. Mum had always been thoughtful and emotionally supportive of me and as I looked into her eyes that day I thought she was the bravest woman in the world.

Just as I was coming to terms with both my losses, the

hospital delivered another heartbreaking blow. I would not be able to attend my granny's funeral. How could I not be there to say goodbye? If I had had the strength and energy I would have ripped the wires from my body and crawled there. I desperately wanted to say my own farewell to the woman that I loved so deeply. But, someone came up with the bright idea that I should write a poem that could be read out instead. It made me feel that I could add something so that everyone there would know that I was with them in spirit.

It was only a couple of days following my amputation that I sat with a pen and paper trying to write the hardest words. How could I sum up this amazing lady and how life would be now she was gone in a few words? I managed a poem and my last words to my granny. It was an emotional farewell eulogy, but looking back I wonder whether at the time I actually believed she was gone. I wasn't able to say goodbye and it all seemed unreal somehow. I couldn't cry either. My family came to visit me and Mum gave me a small brown box. When I was growing up, granny had always told me that the gold sovereign on a chain that was hers would be mine one day. That day had come and

sitting there I opened the small box to reveal the last thing that my granny would give me.

After they had all gone I sat alone with the sovereign placed delicately around my neck. It was then, staring out of the window that the overwhelming feeling of loneliness became acute and the tears came then thick and fast. I cried for so many things. I cried because granny was gone and I couldn't be there to say goodbye. I sobbed because I resented the fact that everyone else who wanted to attend her funeral could go and I cried some tears for the new me that looked so different from before. I still hadn't managed to pluck up the courage to look and as I held the sovereign tightly I cried myself to sleep knowing life would never be the same again.

As the days passed I was determined that I was going to get better. Across the ward from me lay Marjorie who was doing really well with her own recuperation. We decided to have a competition to see who could be the first to do or achieve something new. She pipped me to the post in looking at the stump. It gave me a bit of a kick up the backside to be honest and so that morning when it was time to wash my "undercarriage" I decided enough was

ABOVE

All snug – me as a baby,
wrapped in a blanket.

RIGHT

Young family – Mum and Dad
posing with me and my
younger brother Chris.

ABOVE

Me aged three,
posing in a chair.

RIGHT

Chris and me in the
garden, on a bike.

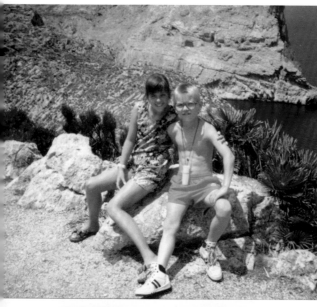

LEFT

Our first holiday
abroad, aged nine
with Chris.

BELOW

Me and Granny.

ABOVE

Posing, aged ten.

RIGHT

Aged nine, beauty
contest photo.

ABOVE

My School Year (always
loved school).

ABOVE

Following my tumour removal, scar through the foot and rash from radiotherapy.

RIGHT

My first amputation – left, below the knee at Treliske Hospital, Truro.

LEFT

Throwing myself
into rehabilitation
(balancing on one leg –
what skill!).

BELOW

Following my first below
the knee amputation.

LEFT

Mum and me at the wedding, wearing my boot.

LEFT

At Auntie's Wedding, Mum Granny and me.

BELOW

In between operations, it was always important to enjoy life, here with Paul.

So in love – my amazing
parents who are always
there 'Team Grose'!

enough. Mum had already admitted to me a few nights before that my family had all had a peek under the blanket the night I came back from theatre. Then it was my turn.

As they peeled back my bedding I turned my head to one side and as I was being washed I gazed at the right area. I was trying hard not to look at my stump directly – don't ask me why, perhaps I was scared – but it seemed right to focus my eyes around the area. I could see from the corner of my eye that it didn't look too bad so I thought I'd have a proper look. For some reason I wasn't particularly shocked. The stump was well bandaged and from what I could see it looked as though I had a fair bit of leg remaining. I had done it! I had faced a huge hurdle and having faced one major challenge I was ready for the next.

But again, Marjorie pipped me past the finishing line. She was the first out of the two of us to lift her stump. She was truly an amazing woman and gave me just the drive I needed. Marjorie giggled as she lifted her stump up high, while mine seemed to have invisible weights attached all around it that that made it swollen, heavy and painful. The thought of moving it was simply unbearable. The third

challenge was to see who would receive the most get well cards. I gloated as my pile of cards was bigger than hers but we stuck all the cards around the ward to brighten the place up.

I was lucky. Each day there would be about eight people sat around my bed. There were family, friends and colleagues and even people who used to live in the same village would pop by. Whether that was out of sympathy or morbid curiosity I wasn't sure, but I was certainly overwhelmed with the numbers of people that visited and I think it helped speed up my recovery. Isn't it strange that when you feel at your most poorly you receive the most chocolates and sweets? I had about 15 boxes of chocolates, teddy bears, balloons and bath salts. The list of get well presents was endless – but Chris was on hand to help and I think he quite enjoyed visiting me and scoffing the chocolates. I was open with everyone and any questions I was asked I tried to answer them as honestly as I could. I even asked my visitors if they wanted to look at my stump! That way it was easier than when people would just sit and stare at the blanket and I knew they were wondering what it looked like.

JUST A *Step*

It had been a few days now and Paul still hadn't looked at it. It worried me as I wondered whether he would really be okay with everything in the end. Would he think less of me as a woman? Would he want to stay with me now? I had many other questions going around in my head as he made various excuses as to why he shouldn't look. But, the following day the decision was taken out of both our hands as the ward staff had finally managed to get me out of bed. I sat in a chair by the bed and began to feel slightly more human again. I even had some soup for lunch!

I knew and felt that I needed to do something to make myself feel better and that afternoon, mum helped me clean my teeth and she battled with my greasy tangled hair that had laid flat and lifeless under me for the last few days. The dry shampoo was applied copiously and within half an hour I looked more like a human being again. I had the full works as mum gently washed my face with a flannel and I applied girly things like lip balm to pep me up and, for the first time in over a week, I sprayed on some perfume. Now, I realise that the state I was in before we started the clean up makes me sound quite disgusting, but honestly, being ill I just didn't care, although when I did

finally get around to it I did feel that bit better.

So, there I was, sitting in the chair beside my bed with my stump on a special rest, hair brushed and awaiting visitors as Paul entered the ward, unaware that I was out of my "pit" and displaying my new look. I knew he'd find it difficult and had struggled to sit with me while I watched *Holby City* or any other hospital drama. This was going to be hard for him.

He walked towards me with a straight face, trying desperately to look into mine. He sat on the bed and held my hand. "Are you okay?" I asked him nervously. "I'm fine," was his response and he got braver when his eyes moved towards my stump. It was heavily bandaged so there was nothing particularly gory about it, but some of the leg and the foot that had once been there was now gone. I felt massive relief when Paul looked. It had been very important for me that he look – with his, and my family's support I felt everything was going to be okay.

Later that evening my dad arrived after work as did Chris and I felt safe surrounded by my family. But, there was underlying sadness. The following day it was my granny's funeral. When I had discovered when the funeral

would be I had immediately asked the nurses if I could go. I had to be there. I had to say my goodbyes, I was her granddaughter. I was swiftly told that under no circumstances would I be allowed to leave the hospital to attend. I felt I was letting granny down. She had been my eager audience on many occasions whenever I wanted to read or tell her about a poem I'd written. I lay in bed and my head filled with happy memories of the amazing woman that I desperately loved. But I was also feeling sad. She felt close though, and I felt as if she were near me, supporting me through my hard time. I just wanted her to hold me. I wanted to smell the talcum powder in her hair and more than anything, I wanted her to tell me that everything was alright.

As suggested, I began writing something for the funeral and although writing about her was hard, there was also something therapeutic about it and I wanted everyone at the service to know that although I couldn't be there, she meant the world to me. I handed the finished words to my mum who kissed me on the head before she cuddled me. I knew I wouldn't now see my family until the following evening and by that time it would all be over. It was

worrying me that I wouldn't be there for my mum and I felt I was letting her down too. I wanted to be there to hold her hand and help her get through the day. Mum was grieving for her own mother and remaining strong for me at the same time. She must have been in agony. As they left, the ward lights were turned down and as one by one the other patients fell asleep I just sat there. Marjorie – as much of a support as ever – whispered across to me. "Are you okay, my love?" she asked. She was well aware of what was going on and over the course of the past few days we had become close. Like people pulling together in a disaster movie I felt she was there for me and on my side. "I'm okay Marjorie, thank you…sweet dreams," I whispered back.

The following morning was particularly tough. I felt as if I were in a daze and all I could think about was what was happening at home. I wondered how my family were coping and I still felt I should be there. I think, looking back, that that day was one of the loneliest days I've ever had. It really hit home that I had lost two massive things; part of my body and part of my heart.

I held tight in my hands the sovereign necklace that

mum had given me. I put it on and it helped me feel closer to everyone. The nurses left me alone during the morning – it was well known I don't like mornings – and they were also aware of what the day meant to me. They would appear each morning at 6.00am with a hover and the breakfast trolley, expecting patients to be wide awake and full of beans. They turn on the ward light full strength and start talking loudly. It would force you to open your eyes. I hated the routine and when they came round with breakfast and shrieked: "What would you like, Leanne?" I would always whimper: "Nothing, thank you," and promptly pull the covers back over my head.

The morning of the funeral they hadn't woken me. They'd let me sleep and when I woke sometime later it was for tablets and a wash. The physiotherapist also made a visit, then I was left alone and I was grateful. My bed by the window enabled me to look outside and it was clear day. I remember thinking more of granny and with the sovereign placed firmly around my neck I thought about everything she had done for me and how we were so alike. My head recounted all the fun we'd had, the holidays she'd been on with us and how she'd taken us into town on

the bus. We'd have fish and chips for lunch and then we'd go to Woolworth's where we could choose something we wanted. Then there would be sweets for the bus ride home. The tears started to roll down my face as I remembered the things we'd shared. The morning was dragging, but I felt like I was in a bubble – I didn't want to be disturbed – which was unlike me. Usually, I'd be the one telling jokes or chatting to everyone else's visitors and other patients, but today I wanted to be selfish and cocooned in my bubble. I was thinking of those I loved.

The late afternoon brought my first visitor. It was the vicar, Bev, who had taken granny's funeral service. I'd met Bev at a funeral I'd been to a while back and she was the first female vicar I'd come across. After the funeral we'd found ourselves eating cake and having a coffee and as we chatted it was clear that we would get on. "Bev, the Rev" I called her and I had asked if she would conduct granny's funeral. She had never met Kathleen Vaughan, my granny, but after talking to me she agreed to take the service. She had come straight from the service to see me and as she came closer she held out her arms. She hugged me and I wept.

I wanted to know how it had gone? I thought if I knew every detail then it would be just as if I'd been there. She told me the place was packed and it made me happy to think that so many people had been there. She said she had read my words. "How's my mum?" I asked. I'd been thinking of her too all day and I was longing to hold her. I knew mum wouldn't think I'd let her down, but that's how it felt to me. "She's okay…she's holding it together," she said as she held my hand tightly. Bev then pulled the curtains around my bed and asked if I would like a prayer.

As I've already mentioned I did go to Sunday school when I was younger, but during my teenage years I would only say prayers if I felt I needed too. However, I still believed and I found it comforting to think there was a God and that he was with me, watching over me. Though, with what I'd been through there were times when it was hard to believe. I held Bev's hand tightly and closed my eyes as she asked God to watch over me and my family. She prayed for me to get better and to bless granny and look after her. I find it hard to understand how some people don't believe. That prayer was the most comforting thing that could have happened to me at that time. I

hugged Bev and thank her for all that she had done for us.

We chatted for a while and her being there brought about a change in me. She had helped me out of the gloomy state – and the bubble – that I had spent all day in. Something you might have gathered by now is that I'm good at wearing a "mask". I don't like anyone to see how upset or worried I can be as I don't want to burden them or make them upset themselves. This bloody smiley mask thing is a bane for me though and I can never shake it off. My family arrived together and I was over the moon to see them. I felt as if I hadn't seen them for a long time and I clung to my mum when she reached me. I noticed how tired they all looked and could only imagine all that they'd been through that day. We have always been a close family and I felt as if I'd been robbed. Robbed of the chance to say my own goodbyes in person to my granny and robbed of the chance to be with my own family at a time when I felt that we all needed to be together. I wanted to know everything as they all relayed the events of the day including who had been at the service. Mum had a small flower in her hand. She had brought it for me. It was one of the flowers that had been in an arrangement for the

funeral. That small flower meant so much, just then.

My family didn't stay long that evening as I told them I was okay and I wanted them to go home. They were obviously all exhausted and I mustered my best smile – there's that mask again – and said it was fine with me if they left. I was okay. They all kissed me and as was usual turned around to wave at the ward door. I kept smiling until I knew they were gone. The tears then hit me and I sobbed uncontrollably. I was feeling sorry for myself. I was feeling sorry for them. I felt like the world – my world – was falling apart and I rolled, in pain, on one side. I still had an epidural pump in my spine and I was careful not to knock the drips and various other tubes as the ward lights suddenly dimmed. I was in relative darkness, I was alone again and I wept, wondering if life would ever be good again.

I spent most of the night sobbing to myself and when morning arrived I decided to give myself a "kick up the backside." I had felt sorry for myself for just one day, but I decided that one day was long enough. I needed to pull myself together before visiting time later on. For once I did "get up" early and to the surprise of the nurses I

agreed to have breakfast. Yes, it was early, but today would be a special day. It was the day I was going to be moved. The physiotherapist arrived bright and early and told me the plan was to get me out of bed and into a wheelchair. It would take me eventually down to the physiotherapy department. To me, they might have well as asked me to climb Mount Everest as it appeared a seemingly impossible task. But I didn't want to moan and I wanted to achieve something amazing. The quicker I got moving – I reasoned – the quicker I could go home.

As usual the nurses came by to wash me but they presented me with an unwelcome surprise. They wanted to change my bandages. I had previously thought I was prepared for seeing what lay beneath them, as I had mulled over the fact that it couldn't be worse than just seeing that my leg had gone – could it? Wrong! Too late, I discovered. As they unravelled the bandages on my stump I began to feel quite scared and panicky. I could feel the stitches pulling at the dry blood and it stung as they gently tried to tug the material free. I closed my eyes tightly as my scar was exposed. I felt afraid to look down, but eventually, taking the proverbial "bullet between my

teeth" I peeked. It looked bloody awful! I had around 50 black stitches around the edge of the scar and a big grip – that I can only describe as a huge bulldog clip – holding the end all together. I couldn't look at the stump scar though – that would come later.

By way of preparation I had been given painkillers around 30 minutes before I was lifted into the wheelchair and I was nervous as four members of staff came towards me. It was like a military operation as I was told what position to be in and at what time. Then there was the infamous countdown. "Okay, Leanne…in, one…two…three…GO!" I was shrieking in pain as the four of them – for whom I felt sorry – used all their strength to get me upright. I was in agony. The agonies of before seemed pathetic compared to the pain I now felt. It was if all the blood in my body had rushed to the end of my stump and I felt as if the stitches would burst. "Okay, Leanne…now we're going to get you in the chair, ready…one…two…three." By now I was really screaming in pain. "Sorry….I'm so sorry…sorry everyone." I was apologising again. I hate to put people out and I didn't want to let everyone down with my yelling and the fact I

was getting upset. As they managed to finally get me in the chair, my nightdress was wet through. I was, by this time, crying and sweating profusely. I felt uncomfortable and my catheter was pulling while other tubes were quickly being untangled by staff. I sat and tried to regain some composure. I was left in the chair for around 15 minutes so that I could settle myself and resemble a calmer person before the physiotherapists came to get me.

When I was wheeled out of the ward I felt free and normal for a moment. In the physiotherapy department, two lovely girls explained that over the next few days they wanted me out of the chair, standing and doing exercises in preparation for going home. Although to me this sounded like "mission impossible", the words "going home" were quickly etched on my brain and I decided to give it my all. The next few days were difficult as I went literally squirming in my wheelchair to do a few exercises. I was regularly lifting my stump up and down until the big day arrived and we attempted to get me to stand.

The two girls were so supportive – literally – as they stood either side of me and I focused on dragging myself from the wheelchair – on which I felt I was dependent – to

something so simple, yet so important: standing. I held them both tightly as I looked ahead trying to focus on the bars opposite me. "Come on, Leanne...you can do this," I told myself over and over as it took every muscle in my body to work at the same time. It felt as if I were trying to achieve the impossible, but when I looked up, it had happened. I was standing! It was uncomfortable and sore, but that paled in comparison to the feeling of huge achievement mixed with a strange feeling of normality. I felt like an athlete. Bring on the *Rocky* soundtrack – because that's how I felt. I was preparing for something amazing, I suppose. I was preparing for the rest of my life.

As the days passed I grew stronger and stronger and I couldn't wait for the evening when I would tell my family and friends what I had done. I always wanted to do something more, even something small seemed a giant leap for me and I felt proud of what I had achieved every day. Marjorie, like me, was doing well and we had more competitions. Who'd done the best at physiotherapy and various other things. By this time our families had met many times and everyone seemed to get on well. My paternal grandparents became fond of Marjorie and they

were grateful that I had someone "on the inside" to offer me help and support. She was incredibly good for me and you'd never have guessed there was such a huge age gap between us. Gran and gramps even bought two bouquets of flowers, one for each of us. It was a lovely gesture that we both really appreciated. As further days passed, my strength was increasing and there was more and more talk of me going home. I'd been in hospital for just over three weeks and I missed being at home desperately. I missed the trashy television programmes I was fond of and I missed having a takeaway with Paul on a Saturday night and chatting on the phone to my friends. You name it, I missed it. I craved normality.

After intense talks with occupational therapists, physiotherapists and any other kind of therapist you can think of I was allowed to go home. Marjorie had pipped me to the post on that one and had been discharged a couple of days before. The two days without her were miserable and it made me even more determined to get out of hospital. Before I left, I received a visit from a kind and helpful woman from the local Prosthetic Clinic at the Derriford Hospital in Plymouth. She would make an

appointment for me in a few months' time to see about fitting a prosthetic leg. The thought of it greatly excited me. I mean, the quicker I had it the quicker I'd walk again and the quicker life would be back to normal. Or, would it? When the time came to go I was wheeled out of the ward in a wheelchair. I hugged and kissed all the nurses goodbye and thanked them for absolutely everything they had done for me. I told them I was eternally grateful for their kindness and help and that I would never forget them. For both Marjorie and me they had played a crucial part in our lives. Then, for just a moment, I was filled with panic as I was nervous about leaving and I felt as though I was leaving my comfort zone. But, as I finally made it through the doors of the hospital to the outside world, I left, hoping I'd never have to return there again.

On the drive home, I smiled all the way. This time, it wasn't a mask. Arriving at my house was exciting and the occupational therapist pushed me up the newly fitted ramps to my home. But it looked strange. It wasn't how I remembered it. There was now a single bed in the corner of the living room, a ghastly looking commode in the other corner and there seemed to be ramps everywhere.

"Now, before I leave, I want to make sure you can get around safely," said the occupational therapist in an authoritative tone.

She made me demonstrate how I would move around the house. I felt like a contestant on the *Krypton Factor* and I was worried that one false move over a simple manoeuvre would see me whisked straight back to the nightmare I'd just left. I smiled and promised not to do anything silly – like attempt stairs – for at least a couple of months. I was also not to be left alone for any considerable amount of time. As the door closed behind her the relief I felt was immeasurable.

Paul had to go back to work, so my dad stayed with me and we managed to get me on the sofa. We watched a movie and dad said: "I'm proud of you, Leanne." His words meant so much as he gently touched my leg. I think there's something monumental about your dad telling you he's proud of you. It's easy to forget how difficult it must have been for my parents and I'd often felt like I'd let them down. Dragging them through the trauma I felt guilty. But, my family would be quick to point out what a crazy notion that was.

After a couple of days staying home, still feeling like a patient, I decided that I was fed up with the feeling. I wanted to push myself harder and I reasoned that if I wanted my old life back that I needed a challenge. One day when Paul had left for work, I persuaded everyone else that I'd be okay on my own. After all, I'd only be lying in bed. But, I decided that I wanted to take a bit of a chance. Alone in the house, I wheeled myself over to the stairs. I slowly moved from the wheelchair to the bottom step.Now, I wouldn't recommend this to you, but I slowly managed to pull myself up step by step perching my bum on each one as I got higher and higher. It was against hospital advice. I got into a lot of trouble from my family when they discovered what I'd done. Okay, so it took me what felt like forever, but it was worth reaching the top when I could see my bedroom for the first time in a long time. The pain was horrendous, and had been since I left hospital, but I felt as if I was in the middle of achieving something fantastic. It took all my energy to get into my bedroom and once I was there I lay on the floor in agony. I was there nearly an hour before I had more energy to make it onto the bed. But, the adventure didn't stop there.

LEANNE GROSE

My determination to get well and to improve my stamina and strength saw my first appointment from the prosthetic department at Derriford come through. At last, it felt like other progress was being made and that things were going in the right direction. It wouldn't be long now before I could slip on a piece of plastic which would fit over my tiny limb. I thought I'd be tottering around in high heels before too much longer. For the past few months I'd had the support of my family, friends and colleagues. I'd also had support from strangers, doctors, nurses – everyone had seemed to be there for me. I had received more than 300 get well cards and my living room still resembled a florists. Colleagues from work would often come and sit with me keeping me up-to-date with the gossip and news. I longed for each Friday when dad had the day off so that he could come over and keep me company. Paul was busy at work and because night time was uncomfortable for me, we made up a bed in the spare room so he could get the good night's sleep he needed. My body clock was simply all over the place. I'd sleep in the afternoon, stare at the ceiling through the night and on days when the pain was unbearable, I relied heavily on

morphine. I sometimes felt I was in a permanent comatose state. The night before I was due to go to Derriford, I was bursting with excitement. I hadn't been far in quite a while before then. I'd been cut off at home for some time, so even a trip to the hospital seemed exciting.

I was picked up the following morning by ambulance with a lovely crew who wheeled me into the ambulance and then manoeuvred me onto a stretcher. It was always times like this that I looked awful. My hair was unwashed and I wasn't wearing make-up. So, of course, I'm picked up by the most handsome ambulance crew you can imagine. I was void of all feeling, as it were, I wasn't a young woman in her 20s – I WAS A PATIENT!

Once at Derriford, I met the prosthetic consultant who checked my stump. It was till extremely sore, but I remained positive and upbeat and still believed it wouldn't be long before I was up and walking. I was even more encouraged when I was moved into the casting room and saw several amputees of various ages walking around on false legs. It was actually the first time I'd been together with so many amputees and I couldn't wait to get fitted and be off!

Chapter 5

The last?

It would be several more weeks before I returned to Derriford to be fitted with my exciting new appendage. I had started to feel better in myself and although my stump was still painful I began to feel human again. I had even made several trips into town. As I mentioned at the beginning I'm not known for being shy and retiring, but the first couple of times I went into town, with someone from my family, or a friend, pushing me in my sexy NHS wheelchair, I felt I had lost my identity. I no longer felt like I was me – Leanne. One of the times I was pushed around town I might as well have had two heads due to the number of people staring at me. I think that those very same people must have thought I was blind too. Did they not think I could see them nudging each other? Some would just stare longer than I think is acceptable and I couldn't believe it. Was I really that hideous now?

I soon discovered who the kind people in society are.

Was it teenagers? No, well the elderly then? Forget it. What about those of my age and above? Not on your life. The kindest people I met following my operation were children. I knew instantly that any child would look at me, as obviously I was different from other people around them. The number of children that would approach me and innocently ask what happened to my leg was amazing. At first I was unprepared for their frankness, and to begin with I wasn't sure how to answer. But, I soon became accustomed to the questions and would reply: "My leg was poorly. Hopefully, I'll get another one soon." To my surprise, that was that. They were satisfied with the answer and would let me be. Either that or they were dragged off by a frantic looking parent who would glare at me as though I'd poisoned or tainted their child in some way. I had learned it was simpler to be honest and frank about it and while out and about, I met all types of characters. Children had innocent curiosity. Some people, however, would actually stare at me with their mouths hanging open.

I'd start off by trying to ignore these people. But then I began to stare back at them, muttering under my breath:

"I'm not blind, you know!" which okay might have been a little bit childish, but there was only so much I could take. My time recuperating had allowed me to gain even more strength and the time came to go back to work. Carrick were fantastic about my return and everything had been set up in such a way so as to help me as much as possible. My desk had been raised so that I could get my wheelchair underneath and they had even bought me a special rest to put my stump on. I felt I was truly cared about by my employer. Being back at work also helped with my self-esteem and I felt useful. I'm not saying it was easy – it was anything but – but having a routine definitely helped me mentally and I felt worthwhile. Life, it seemed finally, was getting back to some kind of normality and although the pain was still intense, and getting around was difficult, I was happy and I was alive.

Paul and I both had good jobs. Admittedly, his was a lot higher up the scale than mine, but then, he was older. I worked extremely hard and spent time studying law. Then I landed my dream job in Carrick's human resources department. I became their training co-ordinator. I absolutely loved the job and the people around me. I had

greatly enjoyed the legal department, but people are much more my thing. Human resources gave me the opportunity to blossom and I adored the people I was working with. I found I was working with like-minded people and they became my friends; they were my kind of people. I felt blessed that they had offered me the job, even though I wasn't, at the time, in the best of health and I had never imagined that they would choose the one-legged girl in the wheelchair over all the other fit young applicants. I was reassured that I got the job on my merits. They could see how hard I'd worked in Carrick before and they realised I wouldn't always be like I was.

The head of personnel, Gill, was my boss and she had worked for Carrick for a very long time. She was suffering from breast cancer. She had lost her hair and I was aware that she was receiving daily treatment. Gill was positive and strong. Apart from one man, the whole department was comprised of women and I worked in an office with Charlie and Emma. Both were slightly older than me but we talked about anything and everything – of course, we were working as well! Being part of this team made me feel girly again and I resorted to being the "clown" I'd

always been at school. My confidence, both personally and professionally began to grow. We'd often go out for lunch and neither of them seemed to mind pushing me in my wheelchair. We also didn't need much of an excuse to buy cakes in the afternoons and as the pounds piled on, I really didn't care. I was loving every second of my new-found life. Gill grew very sick, and Jacquie took over as boss. She was good at her job and we had a young, friendly, hard-working team. Jacquie was only 10 years older than me and I think she came across as more of a friend than a boss. It worked for the team and we pulled together in every way possible.

My exciting day for a return trip to Derriford arrived. "Hooray!" I was pleased and had been busy counting down the days. I couldn't wait to pop it on and get back to normal. I really did think it would be that easy. Paul drove me to Plymouth and I was bursting with happiness all the way. However, I was a little apprehensive as I was worried about what it would look like. Would I be able to walk straight away, or would it take me a little while? It felt like I had a million questions all running around in my head. We sat in the waiting room for ages. People were in and out

of the consulting room all the time and I found myself peeking at people's feet to see who had false legs.

"Leanne," Carey, the prosthetics expert called. Carey was young, outgoing and lovely and I felt comfortable with her. She took me to the gym room and I sat on a chair. Paul remained in the waiting room. As usual I wanted to go in on my own. Carey disappeared off to the lab and returned carrying a rather large and bulky prosthetic leg with a tag on it saying "Leanne Grose". I felt a wave of disappointment wash over me at the sight of it. I'd been expecting something that looked, well, nicer for a start, and definitely more human. I suppose I'd blanked out the fact that I would never actually get my leg back and would probably never have something that resembled it and it was just starting to hit me. I tried really hard to smile and as usual made jokes. I managed to make other patients and staff laugh, but the reality was just sinking in. We began with Carey showing me how to put on an "Isros", a latex tubing that slides over your stump. It hurt as I tried sliding it on myself. I gritted my teeth and used all my strength not to cry buckets. It felt like I was ripping my scar. "Come on, Leanne...push!" I screamed as I

eventually pulled it over the swollen part. It attached and was on, and I lay back in the chair sweating and panting. How on earth would I cope with this every day for the rest of my life?

Once the Isros was firmly in place, Carey secured a long bolt at the end of it. This would slot into the prosthetic limb and hold it on. Then the moment came that I will remember forever. I put on the limb for the first time. Two ladies held either side of me and I stood up. My chair was positioned between two parallel bars so I had a safety net all around me. Carey placed the leg under my stump and I had to carefully line the pin at the end of the Isros with the hole within the false leg. Once it was locked, I had to press down with my weight until the leg clicked into place. It was bloody painful and this time I couldn't stop a tear falling from my eye. But, then it was done.

It was on and as the staff stepped back, I could see into the mirror at the end of the bars. ME. Me with what looked like two legs. Okay, it wasn't pretty and the new leg certainly didn't look particularly real. But, as I stood there, still clutching the bars for support, I felt that I had literally taken a giant step. As I continued to stand, the leg felt

desperately heavy. It was like a block of cement pulling me downwards and I won't lie – it hurt like hell. Ignoring the fact I was probably being a fool to even think I had a chance of walking that day, I decided to try. I was expecting miracles as I put my false leg forward. I tried to carry my other leg forward in pursuit, but within a second I knew it wouldn't support me as the pain running through my stump became increasingly more unbearable. I had to stop. But, I was still determined that I wasn't going to give up, even if this was going to be much harder than I'd ever imagined it could be.

"Okay," I told myself, "let's get to the end of the bars." I tried a few steps with this new, alien-like appendage screwed to my poor stump and battled through the pain as I made my way down the parallel bars. I found straight away that I could hardly put any weight through it at all, which was breaking my heart, but I had to remain positive and I kept telling myself that it would "Just take time…it will just take time." I got to the end of the bars and collapsed on the chair. My head was throbbing from where I had put all my concentration into those few tiny steps. I was gutted by the outcome. Carey was extremely good and

tried to make me feel better. "Take it home," she offered, "and have a good old practice."

She was reassuring, but I forced the smile as we met Paul in the waiting room and she handed him my new leg in a large brown bag. Paul could tell from my silence and gloomy face that I was disappointed. "Well?" he asked eagerly as we got in the car and headed for home. "I can't do it Paul," I cried as I burst into tears. Paul, like Carey, was positive and reassuring. But having talked it through with him briefly, for the next hour I sat in silence on the journey back. Tears were rolling down my face. I felt like a failure and I prayed it wouldn't always be this way. The following morning, I decided not to moan, but to try and remain positive. I would get there eventually, I reasoned.

Over the next few days I got into a routine of getting the leg on. I couldn't quite get it off on my own yet, but I could get it on and that was a big step. I went into work as usual in my wheelchair and tried to do a few steps around the office with crutches held firmly. My colleagues were, as ever, supportive and I wondered if they thought I was being a little pathetic. Maybe they thought I could have tried harder, however, I was putting my heart and my soul

into those few tiny steps.

One evening, my mobile rang and I learnt that Gill was very ill and had been taken into hospital. Immediately, Jacquie, Rachael – another great colleague – and I all went to see her. As we went down onto Lowen – the cancer ward – we were all incredibly shocked to see her looking so desperately poorly. She was badly bruised and as we talked to her it became obvious that she wasn't able to understand everything we were saying to her. It was incredibly sad to see this extremely strong woman looking so ill and vulnerable. Gill had never moaned about her condition and she hadn't mentioned that she was feeling so very ill. I think it came as a huge shock to Jacquie who was a particularly close friend. We were all quiet as we left the hospital that night. The following morning it was work as usual and things were fairly quiet, although Jacquie stayed in constant touch with Gill's daughter.

I had decided to give the leg a break – it was hurting me – and I was bruised and swollen and didn't want any more pain. I thought I would give myself a rest and go back to feeling like me again. You realise that it's only a piece of plastic and will never replace the leg you actually

lost, but I had a feeling that I needed to get used to the fact that I had one leg. I needed to feel proud.

I was working when Jacquie approached me and asked to speak to me for a moment. I had thought she was going to pull me up for talking all morning, but as I entered her office I could see that something was badly wrong. "Gill doesn't have much time left," she tried bravely. "They think about 24 hours." The office was quiet. The rest of the day was surreal and we were all caught up in our own thoughts. I couldn't stop thinking about Gill. I felt close to her, having been through similar frightening experiences. When Gill was head of personnel and I had to let her know that I had an MRI scan appointment we ended up having a moan about it as she knew exactly what I was going through. She had been a rock for me in the office and I didn't want to lose her. I wanted to do something to help her, the way she had me, but like everyone else I felt helpless. The next morning Gill died.

Word of her death soon spread throughout the authority and the day, just like the previous afternoon, was surreal. No one called us that day and no one came to visit or asked for anything. It was if the whole Council had shut

down and was thinking of our office. I felt selfish when I realised for a moment that it could have been me. Isn't it strange how your mind works? I'm not selfish by any stretch of the imagination, but I'm sure that others sometimes put themselves in someone else's shoes just as I did then.

On the day of Gill's funeral, we all held each other and grieved for our friend and colleague. We were at the crematorium and, just as I had at Stephen's funeral some years before, I placed my arms around my friends. Emma, tough as nails, stood beside me. Emma was strong and not one to mince her words. From the outside you wouldn't believe that anything could make her cry, but that day she wept beside me and I hugged her tightly. Charlie, who was always there for me stood the other side. She had become my best friend. After that, work just wasn't the same. One of us was gone. As well as losing a friend, I felt as if I'd lost the one person who understood what I was going through. Although all my other friends and colleagues were continually supportive, I knew that I'd particularly miss Gill's support.

As the days wore on, I tried again with the flipping leg.

LEANNE GROSE

I was determined I'd walk. I was fed up with using the crutches and even though I was lucky and had a new flashy purple electric wheelchair – I picked the colour, I might add – things were quite tough. One Sunday afternoon, Paul and I were pottering in the house. We'd recently come back from his parents' house so we could watch Arsenal on the TV. The phone rang. "Hello," I said. "Hi," said a voice. "Is that Leanne?" The lady on the other end had a Geordie accent. "Yes…hi," I replied. "Leanne, darling…it's Heather…Heather Mills McCartney." Well, I wasn't accustomed to phone calls like this and for one moment I wondered if someone was trying to wind me up. But as Heather continued I knew it was her, for real. As it turned out, an old boss of mine was great friends with Paul McCartney's cousin. My former boss had spoken about me and they had asked Heather if she could possibly send me a card or something to wish me well. They had also wanted her to tell me to hang in there with the leg. Heather wanted to speak to me rather than write.

While Paul and his best friend Martin sat on the sofa screaming for the Gunners to score, I was on my bed chatting to Heather Mills McCartney. Okay, perhaps I

would normally have been star struck, but to be honest, after a couple of minutes on the phone I forgot entirely who I was talking to. She was like me – a young woman who'd lost her leg and that was an incredible bond. She didn't seem different at all. She was relaxed and it felt like I'd known her for years as we chatted away and put the world to rights. Heather kindly gave me lots of tips and I found myself explaining about the trouble I was having with my artificial limb. She was actually cooking while she was talking to me and I found her easy to chat to. We said we'd keep in touch and I thanked her for taking the time to call me. It meant a great deal.

Paul was still engrossed in the football when I tried to tell him who'd just rung. I hopped over to the phone and rang my mum who I just knew wasn't going to believe me. I've seen many things in the newspapers, stories on the radio and reports on the television about Heather. But I took her as I found her and I thought she was lovely. After the call I tried to motivate myself again to prove to myself and everyone else I could walk. I'd achieved everything in the past that I'd put my mind to, so why not this?

Dad decided to come with me to one of my walking

sessions. He's been great in the past at encouraging me, whether it was netball, studies or running. He was a great coach and if anyone could help me then he could. I sat at the end of the parallel bars and put the leg on. I managed to do this myself which was a good start and as I made my way down the bars, I had definitely made some kind of improvement but I was nowhere near taking independent steps. "Come on Leanne," said dad patiently, who along with the physiotherapist, was carefully watching every move. I tried, I really did, but I couldn't explain to anyone – doctors, family or friends – why I couldn't do it. I even began to resent seeing lovely old ladies walking around on false limbs and it was painful for me to watch them without feeling like a failure.

I sobbed all the way home from Plymouth with my leg stuffed into a paper bag like a useless old shoe. Dad talked to me and tried to calm me down, but it was no good, I felt useless and like I just hadn't tried hard enough. "What is it Leanne?" he asked. He wanted me to explain why it wasn't happening for me, but the truth is I didn't really know the answer. I could swear that everyone around me thought I wasn't trying hard enough, even though they

weren't about to admit it. At that point, I thought I had let everyone down, including myself. "It's just so painful," I said. I had wanted him to be proud of me that day and while he'd helped patiently at the hospital I felt he was willing me to do something I found impossible. I can be a massive baby at times, but I'd always thought my pain threshold was quite high. But the pain from walking on the prosthetic limb was unbearable. Every time I wore it I felt like I was walking on broken glass.

The following morning I looked at my leg and felt nothing but frustration. I decided not to wear it that day into work and I think my colleagues thought I'd given up. Maybe, at that point, I had, but no one was more frustrated with me than I was. As the day progressed, the ever-present pain in my stump grew worse and worse. "Surely it shouldn't be hurting this badly?" I thought to myself. I put it down to "walking" the day before. The pain was increasingly steadily throughout the afternoon and it was a real struggle to make it to the end of the working day. I was taking more and more painkillers and this in turn made me tired. My days were a long battle. Finally, when it was time to go home, I climbed into bed. I didn't

worry about the evening meal and I didn't even worry about my daily phone call to my parents.

Behind closed doors I could be myself. The mask had gone as I crawled up the stairs and dragged myself across the landing into bed. Within a few minutes I was asleep, the pain and the drugs had exhausted me, and I had been trying so hard, for so long, not to tell my family or my work colleagues. I wanted them all to think that everything was okay and that, although I wasn't walking, despite such a huge operation I was coping.

When I'd been asleep for what only felt like a few seconds I awoke with a jolt. My stump had started to tremble independently and the pain was literally unbearable. I felt sick and was fighting it back, trying not to throw up all over myself. There was no one else in the house and I started to panic. It's hard to put it into words, but it felt as if my leg had been ripped off without an anaesthetic and the muscles were clenching uncontrollably. I used all the energy I had to unclench the muscles, but they were a force to be reckoned with. The pain was so terrible that I began to drift in and out of consciousness and the next thing I knew it was morning.

I was aching deep inside and was so frightened by the

previous evening's experience that I took getting ready for work very slowly. I didn't hop around as I'd tended to do and I used my crutches and didn't even wash my hair. Not washing my hair is a massive thing for me. I managed to put on a little make-up. I've always found that the way I look reflects the way I feel and the more glamorous I felt, the sparkly necklaces, the higher the heel and the heavier the make-up the better. Maybe it was all fake and maybe, just maybe, I didn't just put on the mask for others. Maybe I'd been kidding myself. I continued to think about it as I went into work. The first thing I did when I arrived was to call my surgeon's secretary. Eileen was a lovely lady who was always helpful and kind. I always felt rather guilty about calling as I didn't want to pester her and I knew she had a great many other patients to deal with, but that morning I had no option.

"Eileen? It's Leanne…Leanne Grose." I always wanted them to know me as me and not as my hospital number. After all, I was a person and I had a name. I always got the impression that they were kinder with names than with numbers and I was far from formal with anyone. The staff at the hospital had seen me laugh and they'd seen me cry

and I think any type of dignity goes out of the window when strangers have put tubes inside you, sawn off parts of your body and witnessed you wetting the hospital bed. Yes, that's all me!

"Yes, my love," Eileen replied gently, "what can I do to help?" "I need to see Mr Davies," I said. "I'm sorry Eileen, but I need to see him urgently." I could barely finish the sentence as the tears began to roll down my face. I completely broke down. "I am in so much pain I don't know what to do with myself. I'm desperate," I finished. And, I truly was. In her usual efficient manner she immediately booked me in for a follow-up MRI scan. Although the thought of it petrified me, there was also a sense of relief that something was being sorted sooner rather than later and that they would prescribe some sort of pill to rid me of my miserable despair.

I even found myself smiling as I was pushed down to the MRI scan room just a few days later. As usual I had opted to go alone and I wanted to get it all over and done with as soon as possible, but as I sat in the waiting room, my palms began sweating and I was scared. This time the scan was in the hospital building itself and although it

might sound strange I found it more comforting. The staff were very different in their approach from before and a kind man showed me to a booth where I could change. As instructed, I removed my clothes, underwear, make-up and jewellery and wore the gown provided. I was allowed to use my crutches to get to the actual room itself, but then they had to remain outside the room.

The machine is basically a giant magnet and there are strict rules about what goes on and what you can wear. Two members of staff held me either side and helped me to hop onto the bed. This was, by now, quite familiar territory and a place where I was uncomfortable and afraid. I lay on the bed and as the two staff, a man and a woman, were busy strapping my body and placing foam under my stump, I stared at the ceiling and my eyes glazed over. "Are you okay, Leanne?" the young man asked. "I'm so sorry. I'm so sorry to be like this," I replied, "I'm so scared" and with that I began to cry. He put his hand on my arm. "You'll be fine…we'll get this over with as soon as possible, and I promise to talk you through it all on the headphones right the way through." "Thank you…thank you so much…I don't mean to be such a baby," I said as they left

the room to go next door to their room. And, there I was. Alone again. I stared at the ceiling as the bed moved further into the machine. I held my breath, afraid to move and I tried to tell myself this time it would be different. It was down to me alone to make this more bearable. I had to be strong and my tears weren't really helping the situation.

Around 40 minutes later I was still lying, strapped to the bed and buried deep inside the tunnel which I feared so much. Then finally a voice came through the headphones. "Leanne, we are coming in to give you a small injection." My body went numb. This time I knew what to expect and I tried to brace myself for what was about to happen. I think at least with this scan I was informed all the way along about what was happening and I think before that the fear of the unknown had made it so unbearable. The staff, this time, treated me like a human being and while I was afraid of the ladies in the portable building where the first scan took place, I felt much more safe with the staff here, no matter how scared I truly was.

They entered the room and it was once again like a military operation. I was pulled out from the machine and

they quickly put a tourniquet tightly around my right arm. I knew it would hurt – my previous experience had taught me that – but I knew deep down that the quicker it was done then the quicker I could get home. It took several minutes for them to be able to find a vein, which isn't ideal when you're petrified of needles, and I turned my head away determined not to look. "Sharp scratch," the man said as I felt the end of the needle pierce my skin. I took a sharp intake of breath. "Is it in now? Is it over?" I said panicking as it stung like mad. "Sorry, Leanne...we lost the vein. We are going to try again." Three attempts later and they hadn't managed to find my delinquent vein. "We're going to call a doctor over...he'll be able to do it in no time." Was it just me, or was this *déjà vu?* I felt sick to my stomach.

The doctor who arrived was great and very gently managed to hit the right spot. It was in. I let out a massive sigh of relief and psyched myself up for round two in the machine. "Okay, Leanne...just one more scan left, just stay still." For some strange reason, knowing that the needle was in and that part was over made the last few minutes more bearable and eventually, it was over. Hearing them

come into the room, I felt like they were coming to rescue me and as they helped me from the bed I broke down again. I kept apologising for being such a problem patient and I hugged them as I left. Like before, I didn't even think about the results. I was just so relieved that the blasted scan was over. I couldn't wait to go home and cuddle up with my family. I was a little surprised, however, when a few days later, there was a call from the hospital to ask me to meet with my surgeon. He was such a kind man. He had carried out the amputation and he was someone I truly trusted. He'd always supported me and I felt close to him. With him, I felt more than a number and I felt he really did care.

Going into his office I was cracking jokes and trying not to think about the horrendous pain I was still going through. I couldn't wait for him to come up with a magical cure. As I sat there I noticed that he looked deep in thought and I immediately realised that something was wrong. He was polite and asked how I was doing and I just knew he was stalling for time. "Leanne," he said eventually, "The scan revealed something else." My heart was now in my stomach and I felt sick. "There's a shadow

in your stump and we think that it may be what you had last time." The strange thing was that I wanted to make him feel better. "Okay," I responded, "so, what are we going to do about it?" I thought he was about to suggest another round of radiotherapy or something along those lines.

"I've had a meeting about you," he continued, "and, unfortunately, we no longer have the knowledge to treat you down here so I'm sending you to Bristol for another opinion." "Oh," I said. "Okay." My mask was firmly on. "I hope I see you again?" I really didn't want to lose the surgeon I trusted. "You certainly will, Leanne," he replied. "I will get updates on you regularly," he finished as he shook my hand. I wanted, at that minute, to give him a hug. Although I always wanted to go to my appointments alone, I must admit, that right at that minute I found it really hard and I could have done with a hug. I settled for the handshake and looked into his eyes telling him I was scared. I headed for the nearest toilet where I began to cry. What had I done to deserve this? I'd been through enough. Surely I wouldn't be put through more?

I wiped my tears and looked into the mirror. I looked

at myself and told myself I would be strong. I could beat this. It wouldn't be that bad. It couldn't be any worse than what I was imagining, could it? I relayed the news to my family and friends and, as was usual, they got the edited down version. They didn't need to know all the gory details and it was far kinder on them if I heard the news first, digested it and then put on the pretence that I was coping. Maybe that's wrong, but it was my coping mechanism and I wanted to cope for them too.

Within a couple of weeks I was on my way to Bristol. Paul came with me but I told my parents we'd be okay on our own and that I was absolutely fine. The journey was only a couple of hours or so and it was only a day appointment. I don't know why, but I always found that if I knew I was going in and straight out again it made me feel a lot more at ease. As we arrived at the hospital it felt strange being somewhere else. The surroundings, of course, were completely different from the Royal Cornwall Hospital, and I didn't know anyone. I was out of my comfort zone.

I said goodbye to Paul in the hospital canteen and left him reading a magazine as I made my way to the waiting

room. I was introduced to the consultant specialist to whom I took an instant dislike. Although it was unlike me to dislike someone straight away, he appeared very stern and was even quite cold towards me. He was totally matter of fact and asked me to lie on the bed so he could take a good look at my stump. After a couple of minutes of poking and prodding it, he sat me up and said that he wanted to operate the next day. "Operate?" I couldn't believe it and I looked at him in disbelief. "Yes, we will take you to theatre and do a biopsy...you will need to stay in a ward tonight and I will see you tomorrow." And, with that, he was gone. I sat still on the bed with my eyes glazing over.

"My mum," I suddenly said. "Can I ring my mum?" The nurse in the corner of the room showed me to another office and I felt pathetic as I was ushered through the crowded waiting room, shaking and stuttering. In the privacy of the room provided I rang my mum. While I waited for her to answer I was desperately thinking of how to put things so she wouldn't worry. I wanted to do the "usual" and make her believe I was okay but my plan failed miserably. I wailed down the phone at her: "Mum...they're going to operate tomorrow." I could tell within seconds

that I'd made a mistake getting so upset. I could hear the panic in her voice and I wanted to protect her from it. "We're coming up," she said firmly. "No...it's okay mum," I lied through my teeth. "I don't care Leanne...we're coming up," she repeated in a firmer tone. "There's no point in arguing..." "Okay," I interrupted. I didn't care anymore. I was too tired to fight and I actually just wanted them there. I went to find Paul to tell him what had happened and then we were shown to the ward. It all seemed a bit surreal and I just couldn't take in what was happening. I then begged the hospital to let me out that evening and I promised I'd be back early for the procedure.

Paul and I found the nearest hotel and were barely able to speak as we both knew what each other was thinking. We were going to go through all the heartache again. About three hours later, my parents met us at the hotel. We all hugged as if we hadn't seen each other in years. I think we all felt relieved to be together. Paul and dad decided that it would be better if we didn't just dwell on what was happening and we all went out for a meal. As of midnight there would be no eating and drinking for me

and I took myself off to bed trying really hard not to think about what would shortly be happening. The alarm on the hotel television sounded the following morning and for a brief second I had forgotten why I was there. I put on my "face" and decided to get on with it. We met my parents in the lobby and I reassured them I was okay. I was trying to convince each and every one of us. Once in my hospital bed, I met the nurses and got into my gown. It took me right back to that frightening day when they took my leg away. I hated the waiting and made a trip to the toilets. My mum came with me and helped me into the wheelchair that was provided. My stump was by now so incredibly painful and I think, however silly this might sound, that it knew what was happening as it shook like crazy.

Mum wheeled me into the cubicle where I sat on the loo. I asked her to face the corner as I covered my modesty. "Everything will be alright, darling," she said as she faced the toilet wall. I started to cry. "I'm just in so much pain mum, I can't stick this pain...I can't put up with much more." She left the corner where I'd ordered her to stand and came over and hugged me as we sobbed together.

Together as I sat on the loo, no mask now, she could see the real me for a change. I felt like a small child again in her arms and in so many ways I wished I still was. Back when I was little with no worries, I could run and play with my friends. That was a time before fear and pain when a hug from mum, over a grazed knee, would make everything alright again. I knew she felt helpless, but that hug and the love and support she had, that she was continuing to give me was what I needed. We both dried our tears and then mum wheeled me back to the ward where we all continued to wait.

I was collected by porters and taken to theatre. I had an overwhelming feeling of *déjà vu* and collectively we took an intake of breath. After the operation, as before, the relief was immense. The feeling of being alive and that I'd survived was fantastic. But, compared to other operations, this procedure had been relatively small and I realised that maybe I had worried a little too much – maybe I was even becoming a bit braver. Shortly after I was taken back to the ward where mum, dad and Paul were told they could prepare to take me back home. I was taken to the car in a wheelchair and although my stump was bandaged

following the biopsy I could see a big arrow drawn with a thick marker pen – obviously to tell them which side to work on.

I travelled back in mum and dad's car and the journey was horrendous. Dad tried to make it as comfortable as possible for me by laying out cushions and a blanket. But every bump in the road made me wince and every corner made me squeal. By the time we, and Paul in the car behind, got home I was emotionally and physically shattered. Paul and I decided to stay with my parents that night and it was good to see Chris and update him on what had happened. I loved it when we were all together. "Team Grose" I like to call us and that's exactly what we were – a team. But we all had different roles.

Dad was the strength that held us all together; the sensible one, the protector. Mum was the loving one who'd be there for cuddles and kisses and mopping up tears. Chrissy would keep us all entertained with tales of his exploits and his news about what he was doing brought a sense of normality to things. But sometimes, since I'd been ill, I sensed that he felt a bit guilty. We'd grown up enjoying sports, running around and he knew I could no

longer participate. I think that it affected him more than he let on. And, darling Paul – the one who made me laugh – my rock and the one to pick me up and never let me feel sorry for myself. All these roles were important and I was grateful to be on such a winning side.

As I couldn't make it up the stairs that night mum made a bed on the sofa in the living room. I said it would be fine. However, going to the loo – to be blunt – was going to be more of an issue. Needs must though and mum helped me to pee in a jug. Okay, it might not have been very ladylike, but when you've got to pee, you've got to pee! It's strange, but when you're in pain you don't really care about the etiquette of it all and I was, after all, with my mum. I managed to get to the kitchen while all the boys were under strict instructions to remain where they were – I wasn't going to completely lose all modesty! Mum helped me position the jug between my legs and as I started to pee into the jug, even though the pain was horrendous, mum and I started to giggle. We were uncontrollable and to be honest, I'm not really sure that we knew what we were laughing about. But we didn't care. It relieved the pressure in more ways than one and it was a

nice moment between us – the laughter, the closeness and the pee in a jug!

When everyone had gone to bed, I lay on the sofa in the dark with my eyes wide open. It was the first time I'd had to myself and things were starting to sink in. I asked myself the questions I'd asked before and I prayed that the tumour hadn't returned. I had a couple of days to recover from the biopsy in Bristol before I was called back to the Royal Cornwall Hospital. This time I did let Paul come with me, but again, I asked him to stay in the waiting room while I went in to hear the verdict. "Okay, Leanne," said my consultant. He was his usual gentle self, but as before, he looked serious. "We've had several meetings here and a lot of specialists have looked at your scans," he continued. "We aren't really sure what exactly it is but, it is very, very rare and we think that your tumour is back…it's been decided to send you to a hospital in London to see a top consultant." My heart sank and I suddenly felt very sick. "I have to go to London?" I asked, dreading the response. "You will get the best care Leanne…it's in your best interests and we need to get this sorted." I didn't know what was worse, the fact that I still had some vile alien

thing growing inside my body or, the prospect of going to London.

Since I was little I had had a real fear of London. I'm not exactly sure why, but I thought it was frightening and scary. I had a lot of fears and the events of 11 September 2001 had made me feel all the more anxious about going. I believed everything in the news and on TV and it just seemed like a million miles from Cornwall. A million miles from home. After pleading my case to Mr Davies, he assured me that there was no other option. He was sending me to see the very best consultant and if I cared about my health I would go. Although I was petrified I didn't really have any choice. He tried to reassure me that I would be fine and in the safest hands possible. We agreed to disagree and I left his office and headed straight for Paul. "Please take me home," I said quietly. I looked like I'd been knocked backwards. "Babes?" he asked inquisitively. "It's back Paul...it's back and I have to go to London."

Although the pain was unbearable, all I wanted to do was get out of there. I felt sick and panicky as I started to head for the exit on my crutches. There was a muffled

sound behind me and I turned around. I couldn't believe what I was seeing. I was completely taken aback at the sight of Paul, breaking down and crying in the middle of the corridor. He didn't do that. He was the strong one. He was my rock. I went back to him and flung my arms around him tightly. "I'll be fine Paul...I'm not going anywhere," I said as I tried to convince us both. For once it felt real. There was no mask and no false smile. It felt real and that was terrifying. I think you go into some kind of "crisis mode" and during the journey home I decided that however scared I was feeling about going away it wasn't going to affect us or ruin our lives. I kept myself busy during the next couple of weeks before we had to make the journey and I went into work and tried really hard to get everything up to date. I caught up with friends and paid my bills. I answered all outstanding text messages and emails and felt strangely like I might not be coming back. I wanted to tie up all loose ends.

By now it was January and I wanted a fresh start. I'd even backed down about my family all accompanying me to London. Although to be fair I don't think they'd have taken "no" for an answer. It also didn't feel fair to shut

them out and I appreciated they'd worry more being far away. I also didn't think I could go through it alone – not this time and I was even more scared and frightened than before. Before I could think about it the day to go had arrived. Mum, dad, Chris and Paul would all be travelling with me to hospital. Paul, who was originally from Epsom was used to the "Big Smoke", however for the rest of us it was completely new territory.

We arrived at the Stanmore Hospital and were surprised and shocked by how old and dated it looked. As we walked to the ward our jaws almost dropped to the floor as we entered a corridor to the wards which had a massive concrete slope that travelled right up through the hospital. It was like nothing we'd ever seen before and it made us all smile – once we'd got over the shock of it. We found Ward 4, my ward, and as we arrived we were met by the kindest hospital staff you could imagine. They were happy and friendly and instantly made me feel at ease. It was almost as if we weren't in hospital at all and it all felt extremely relaxed. It helped me to feel less nervous. I was told I was having a biopsy in the morning and strangely I began to feel quite comfortable and alright.

Mum, dad, Chris and Paul were all staying onsite which was wonderful for me. I wanted to feel close to them and I was more nervous about how they were going to get on than I was. As they went to unpack in their nearby rooms, I unpacked my bits and pieces and lay quietly on the bed. I was preparing myself for yet another biopsy and as the evening came I met my new surgeon. It was weird to see someone else – I'd been so used to Mr Davies – and this man had my future in his hands. He was a strong-looking man and he instantly made me feel safe. He sat at the end of my bed and smiled as he explained what would be happening to me. I felt that I trusted him. "See you in theatre," he said and he smiled confidently at me as he left.

My previous worries about going to London, meeting new people and the impending surgery began to fade. I began to think of it as having "a job to do." I wanted to get it done and get back home to where my heart belonged – Cornwall. My thoughts were interrupted as my family, who were laughing uncontrollably entered the ward. Having asked me if I was okay and wanting news on what the surgeon had said they then told me what was going on.

They were staying in a horrendous dump nearby. There was no heating, the water from the taps was brown and mum and dad would be sharing a tiny single bed which was apparently filthy. They were still laughing about it and it was refreshing to have something to laugh about instead of worrying for a moment. It would certainly make the trip more memorable. The great thing for me was that I knew they wouldn't care. They had wanted to be with me and they were.

The atmosphere in the ward was fantastic. I'd started to make friends with other patients and I found it comforting that I was surrounded by people in a similar situation to my own. I'd always been told, especially being so young, that my condition was rare. But at Stanmore I was one of many from all over the country and I now believed I was in the best place possible for treatment. We even had "bedtime bingo" which was arranged by the hospital radio station. It was unbelievable. The numbers were called out over the radio and the whole hospital was playing. There was a lot of excitement and we all listened intently as I drank a hot chocolate and we ticked off the numbers on the form. "Bingo!" my mum cried. She'd won

– we shrieked with laughter as a hospital radio mug, pen and bookmark were delivered to my bed. It was great fun and quite surreal at the same time. By the time I went to sleep all thoughts of the following morning had gone and I drifted off to sleep feeling safe in my new surroundings. I think I had a smile on my face and this time it wasn't a mask.

As you know, I'm not good in the mornings but that day I woke immediately as the busy ward began buzzing with activity. I felt positive and had picked myself up from my previously unhappy state. I was unwavering when it came to the thought of getting through it as easily as possible. Although breakfast was a no-go area, I made my way to the loo to freshen up. I simply washed my face – no make-up and hairspray allowed today – and cleaned my teeth without swallowing any water – a definite pre-operation no no. I made myself look really sexy by running a comb through my hair and applying a little dry shampoo. Oh, alright, I looked awful, but at least I'd made the effort. It certainly made me feel a little more human. I hobbled out to the ward and instead of sitting and worrying I made my way around the bed and said hello to everyone.

I almost forgot about my operation as I learnt about the amazing people on the ward with me. Some had been in hospital for such a long time. It also opened my eyes that there were patients there from all over the place and that it wasn't just me that had travelled to be there. I found it refreshing to meet people from all different backgrounds, religions and creeds and no matter how different our lives were away from Stanmore we all had two things in common. We had all suffered from similar illnesses and we had all been in a great deal of pain.

I think my family were a bit surprised to arrive to find me chatting to people rather than shaking on the bed. The atmosphere really suited me and when the porters turned up to collect me for theatre for once I was calm and not paralyzed with fear. As I was pushed down the "slope" of the hospital to the theatre at the bottom of the building my dad was holding my hand. It was the new arrangement. Dad would once again be coming into the anaesthetic room with me. He was strong and would hold it together. Mum would have cried and we decided that Paul would probably pass out. It had only taken 10 minutes for me to feel safe at the Stanmore and so I was feeling

more comfortable than usual which in turn made this the calmest procedure I had gone through up to that point. With the biopsy complete, I was returned to the ward to meet an eager, if somewhat worried, family. The surgery always made me shake a little afterwards, but I knew I was going to be alright. Stanmore had a much more laid back attitude than any of the other hospitals I'd been to and I think it had a calming effect. There were no strict visiting times and family members and other visitors could come and go as they pleased. You could use your mobile phone and the care I received while I was there was absolutely phenomenal. I had begun to feel silly about having worried about coming to the Stanmore – it was such a wonderful place. Within 24 hours the worst was over and I was ready to make the long journey home. I was secretly praying that the results would not be far behind me.

The biopsy itself hadn't been too intrusive and was certainly a more straightforward operation than the actual amputation, so I was soon back at work. It was actually great to be back and it made me feel normal again. It gave me a good reason to get up in the morning, to put on my

"slap" and go and be with my friends and colleagues. Everyone was pleased to see me and the biopsy was soon forgotten about. I've always been able to get over things relatively quickly – even when I received bad news and unwelcome results, it would be awful for a few days, the worst thing in the world even, but then I'd get over it. I didn't want to let things ruin my life and I would try not to dwell on things too much. It's that attitude that's enabled me to cope with the "rollercoaster" of a ride that I've been on.

It was a usual day when I made my way into work one morning. When my leg was amputated, I lost my driving licence for health reasons – which had actually been a devastating blow – so I would either travel with Paul, or if I was going at a different time, I'd travel to work in my wheelchair. It could certainly wake you up in the morning, whizzing along when it was chilly. It was turning into an uneventful day, but I was aware that I hadn't had any news from London. The more colleagues asked me if I'd heard anything, the more nervous I became. After lunch, the phone rang. I picked it up and cheerily asked how I could help. I think my heart skipped a beat when I heard Mr

Davies' voice on the other end. Jacquie and Sandra were not far away and I was conscious of their presence. I didn't want to react whichever way the phone call was going. I wanted to play it cool. Mr Davies was as polite as always but calmly told me the tumour was back.

"Okay," I said and then asked him my standard response. "What are we going to do about it?" I was desperate to know what would be happening to me next and I wanted his reassurance they could do something to help me. "They're going to take away your knee, Leanne," he offered apologetically. "They will amputate just past the knee." "They?" I asked. In a drastic twist, I was hoping against hope that I was going back to London. "Yes, Leanne...you'll be going back to London." I tried with everything I possibly had at that moment not to cry. I didn't think crying was for the office – I knew people would understand – but I didn't want to impose this on them. "Okay, thank you," I replied. I knew I would now have to relay the conversation, but I didn't know if I could tell anyone what I'd just heard.

"Okay, Leanne?" asked Jacquie and Sandra – who were obviously aware of what the phone call was about. Their

faces were full of concern. I put the mask firmly back on. As I smiled, I said: "That was Mr Davies." As if they hadn't already worked that out. "It's back...and they're going to..." I stopped. My bottom lip had started pulling towards the floor and I couldn't say the words out loud. They both moved closer and that made me feel bad. I didn't want to make them feel uncomfortable. "I'm sorry," I said as I put a piece of paper in front of my face and I began to cry. "I'm so sorry...I shouldn't cry, I'm sorry."

"What did he say?" I was asked. "They are going to amputate again...they're going to take away my knee," and with that I broke down completely. Jacquie and Sandra were both incredibly supportive. Jacquie rang Paul and asked him to come to the office. I asked them not to tell Chris who by this time was also working for the authority as I couldn't let him find out through someone else. As I was voicing my concerns about this it dawned on me. How were my family going to cope with this news?

I met Paul in the First Aid room and he held me as I burst into tears. He was hugging me as he reassured me that, as always, we'd get through this. I decided to remain at work and would wait until later to tell my parents the

JUST A *Step*

news I suspected they were dreading. It wasn't fair to ring them at work and no matter how many times they'd said that it would be fine I just knew they'd have to struggle through to the end of the day. It took me the rest of the afternoon to prepare myself to tell my parents. I was feeling guilty again. I felt as if I was letting them down. I was going to put them through this all over again and I knew that they didn't deserve it. I believe in the saying "The more you love, the more you hurt" and I felt it was true in my family's case.

Paul drove me over to see them that evening – the tears were gone and I was ready to face them with my best fake smile. "I spoke to the hospital today," I began. As I relayed what Mr Davies had said, each of their faces said a thousand words. I finished with: "Honestly, I'm okay with all of this...I'm going to be fine and we know how great they (London) are up there. I'm sure this will be the last one." Truth was, I had no idea if it would be the last time, but at that moment, all any of us could do was hope.

Chapter 6

Don't take no

Yet again I spent the next few weeks frantically putting my affairs in order – "Just in case," I told myself. I resurrected the letters that I'd painfully written before the first amputation in case anything should happen and everything and anything that was outstanding was dealt with. In some ways, it gave me some control. It felt like the only control I had. In the days before the operation I even organised a party. After all, I wouldn't be doing much over the coming months and as I looked around the room at the people who had come I felt proud to have so many friends. There were so many people in that room who were special to me and I knew in my heart that my time couldn't be up. I was once again determined to fight. I would do whatever it took. Chris arrived with his new girlfriend Kate, who was a couple of years younger than him. They looked blissfully happy and that made me happy. The party was a fabulous chance to see people and say my

goodbyes, for now. I wasn't sure whether I was imagining it, but when people left, some hugged me so tightly that I wondered if they were scared too.

The last day in the office was very hard. I wanted to go round and say goodbye to people, but I also wanted to ensure that everything was as up to date as it could be. I loved my job and I didn't want to lose it. My job was incredibly important to me. The afternoon, however, was filled with hugs and tears and at 3.00pm we all went into Jacquie's office for a meeting. What I didn't know was that they had bought me an enormous hamper and everything in it was individually wrapped. I was completely overwhelmed. The people I worked with were quite simply amazing friends. Jacquie, Rachael, Melissa, Shena and Sandra were all seated around the table when Charlie brought in the great box. Yes, I had my family, Paul and my childhood friend Nathan – our friendship was as strong as ever. But, I'd like to tell you about Charlie. I'd not known her long and we became close because of working together, but she and I instantly clicked.

Charlie brought out the best in me and she was a simply amazing friend. We were both extremely loud and

could quite often cause a stir in the office with our constant laughing and giggling. We would laugh at anything and everything and we seemed to be able to tell what each other was thinking. I'm sure many people thought we were childish, but it was fun and refreshing. We had a bond and she felt like my older sister. I'd ask her advice and I trusted in what she told me. She wouldn't shy away from telling me off if I'd done something wrong either. I knew that she would have had a hand in picking what was in the hamper so I knew that I'd love what was in it. I was bursting with excitement as I looked at the beautifully wrapped presents. But at that moment, I was conscious that people here cared about me and they were right behind be. Their support was invaluable.

We shrieked with laughter as I opened present after present. There were all the essentials. A manicure set – they knew I loved doing my nails – a large fluffy blanket, Ritz crackers and fruity sweets. There was a beautiful picture of them all in a frame to put beside my hospital bed. Every gift had been carefully chosen and this thoughtfulness made me realise how much I would miss them. I became really emotional when I had to say

goodbye. I hugged each of them tightly and I didn't want to let go. Mr Winskill, the Chief Executive came down to wish me well – it was a lovely gesture – and I felt sad to be leaving my Carrick "family". As I left the building, I turned for a moment, hoping it wouldn't be too long before I'd be back there once more.

That night, Paul and I stayed with mum and dad as we were all leaving really early the next day. Chris and Kate – who was becoming more and more like family – were coming too and I was relieved that, for once, he'd have someone other than the rest of us to support him. He, like me, always put a brave face on things but I knew deep down he found it all incredibly tough and probably had times when he didn't know how to deal with it all. We'd hired a minibus and it was dark when we got up and packed our bags into it. My uncle Darren had kindly offered to drive us all up to London and bring back the minibus. It would mean a 10-hour or so journey for him, but he insisted on doing it. Like the rest of the family, he wanted to do what he could to help. As dad's younger brother, I think the fact that he was helping, probably helped him a little too. I was quite relaxed on the long

journey up and I had reasoned with myself that being scared all the way would only make the length of it more hellish. Darren dropped us off at the hotel where everyone would be staying. Just then there were sirens which made me feel ever so slightly panicky. It was fear of the unknown and in a bizarre twist, I couldn't actually wait to get to the safety of the hospital. We all stayed at the hotel that night and we had fun eating KFC and watching the *X Factor*. We were all snuggled in mum and dad's room and although that kind of evening may sound boring to some, to me it was sheer bliss.

The following morning we all seemed to have serious faces as we made the trip from the hotel to the hospital. It was several bus rides with a lot of bags, but we reached our destination and I was welcomed warmly by the staff on the ward. I was shown to my bed and was pleasantly surprised when they gave the same bed that I'd stayed in for the biopsy. It was only a little thing maybe, but it was all the more comforting for me. Again, the other patients were all friendly and I quickly made friends with two very special women – Evelyn, who must have been in her seventies in the bed opposite mine, and Amy. She was in

the bed next to me and had long fiery red hair and a great London accent. She was around my age and I was relieved to be with two people who knew what I was going through. Family support is amazing, but I don't think they really understand what it's like. How can they? So, to have two people there who knew exactly what it was like was a huge comfort and relief. Mr Cannon and the surgical team came by as I was unpacking. He explained the operation and answered my questions.

Next came the anaesthetist. She was the first female anaesthetist I'd had and she was simply amazing. She listened to me and took on board all the concerns that I had. I explained about being hopeless around needles and I wanted the special baby cream that makes your hand go numb before they even try and insert a needle. I couldn't face them putting in the canular without it. "No problem," she said gently and told me with a smile that she'd look after me the following morning – I believed her. You would have thought I'd be in floods of tears that evening, but I was surprisingly calm. Paul, mum, dad, Chris and Kate all sat around the bed and finished the evening with "bedtime bingo" which once again lightened the mood

and gave us a giggle.

I suppose I was slightly more distant than I might normally have been, but I couldn't quite get it out of my head that maybe, just maybe, it was my last night with them all. I think it was all quite overwhelming for Kate. She and Chris hadn't been together long and she was already in the thick of the drama. I think she could tell how close we all were and I only hope that she found that a good thing. I didn't want them to stay late and encouraged them to go back to the hotel in Stanmore. After all, they had had an emotional day and there was, of course, more to come. There were lots of hugs and kisses that night as they prepared to leave. It was tradition that they wave until the very last minute – until we could no longer see each other. As they made their way down the corridor and out towards the hub of the hospital I could still see their hands waving madly. When they'd gone it gave me some breathing space. I had my own private routine in order to prepare myself for the next day.

I spent a while reading the texts I had received from family, friends and colleagues and replied to them all. I told everyone I was doing okay and that it would soon all

be over. Answering the people back home made me feel a million miles away. I got myself into the bathroom and thoroughly washed my hair. It was going to be quite a while before I would be able to wash it again and I wanted to feel as clean and fresh as possible. I cleaned my teeth had a good wash and put on my favourite nightdress. I then got everything out on the bed that I thought I would need and was quite fussy about where I placed them. After so many operations I think you find your own routine and learn what works for you. I would like to think that each procedure taught me something new and I soon realised that putting my make-up within arms reach on my cabinet was sensible for me. The magazines on the wheelie desk were obvious and stashing sweets, goodies and drinks in the nearby drawer was bloody essential!

As I was preparing to settle down for the night, I watched as Amy's family were kissing her goodnight. She'd been quiet for a while and, although she was friendly, I didn't know whether to push her into a conversation. I decided I needed to make sure she was alright. "Hi, Amy, are you okay?" I ventured tentatively. "I just want to make sure you're alright?" I said as I leaned over my bed. Within

minutes we were chatting like old friends. She explained that they had found a tumour in her foot, just like me, and she was due to have her toe amputated. She'd already had several other operations and combined with the treatment she'd endured Amy had obviously been through the mill. I could completely empathise with her and for a moment I forgot that I had also been through amputation. We shared stories and tips and talked about everything from medication to men, television to treatment. I think that our chat gave us both some comfort and I sleepily lay back knowing I was happy and had made a new friend. I was determined to be strong and determined to get through the situation. It wasn't just about me, it was about all of us and I was the one that could make it better or worse for everyone.

"Leanne, wake up!" I heard a deep voice whisper from the bottom of the bed. It was Saa, the gorgeous nurse who was looking after me. At first I thought he looked intimidating as he was big built and had no hair. He had a thick African accent, but I soon realised he was a big teddy bear who was extremely kind and sweet – although he did like the Maltesers by my bed! For a moment, I

totally forgot where I was and what was about to happen. Then it dawned on me. "Let's get you to the bathroom and get sorted," he said, adding "we need to be ready for when the medical team come." I instantly got up. The journey to theatre had begun. I made my way to the bathroom and cleaned my teeth, without swallowing any water as instructed. I gave my hair one last brush and sat on the loo. Even though I didn't need the loo because I hadn't eaten, but knowing that I was going to have more of my leg removed I would probably need the loo! I sat there quietly and tried to get myself "in the zone". I would probably have laughed at people who said that before – now though, I knew exactly what they meant. I knew that it would be a while before I needed the loo again and the next time I did it would be through a plastic tube. I went back to the darkened ward and back to my bed.

Saa popped his head through the curtains and smiled as he threw a little package my way. I think that both the staff and the other patients knew I had a good sense of humour and I felt comforted that they were prepared to have a laugh and a joke with me. I didn't want to feel ill, so I often didn't act it. I quietly chuckled to myself when

the package was revealed to be a pair of plastic pants. "Very sexy," I whispered back to him. Saa left me to adorn the gorgeous said pants. It felt like wearing a nappy! As I rolled over in bed the pants crackled and I was grateful that no one could see them – even if they could hear them. I slipped into the gown and was ready.

It was still dark outside and I could hear other patients snoring. It was strange for me to think that all over the country, at that precise moment, millions of people were still sound asleep without any cares. Meanwhile, there was me, becoming more and more petrified in a pair of crackling plastic pants. While it was still quiet I lay still. I closed my eyes, put my hands together and I prayed. As I had done once before, I asked God to help me, I asked him to get me through and to look after my family. I also told him I loved granny and I wished she could be there with me so that I could tell her how much I loved her and that I would be alright. I must have drifted off for a little while – the next thing I knew it was daylight and the consultants were on their way.

About four of Mr Cannon's team came and sat around my bed. Within the department, Mr Cannon was God and

the four that sat with me would also help in my surgery and treatment. They were all lovely as they ran through the standard questions, such as "When had I last eaten?" etc. They then put a big black arrow in marker pen on my stump – to show which leg they would be operating on. "Well, if you get that wrong, I'm in trouble!" I joked, trying to ease the atmosphere. They laughed and as they were leaving my family arrived. I could see straight away that they were all full of tension and fronting their best nervous smiles.

"Morning guys…check out my pants!" I said gleefully as I pulled up my NHS gown. They sat around my bed once again. Mum was stroking my head while Paul was chatting to other patients and trying to make them all laugh. I love to be stroked. I love the touch of someone else, I find it so relaxing. The fact that I'd been up at some ridiculous hour, plus mum stroking my head meant that I drifted off to sleep. They all sat quietly around the bed. No one wanted to wake me. The fact I was sleeping meant that I wasn't worrying and so I couldn't get more and more nervous. I was having a lovely dream and then I awoke. I looked straight into my mum's eyes. I stared at her for a

moment; she was standing over me with a worried look. "They are here for you darling," she said. I looked to the foot of my bed and there they were. The two porters that had taken me to theatre the last time. Time to say goodbye – the hard bit.

My brother held me close and kissed me. "Good luck, sis…I love you." "I love you too Chrissy," I said. I was trying not to show any weakness, although by this time I felt as though I was going to throw up all over myself. Kate was in floods of tears as she gave me a cuddle and said good luck. I asked her to look after my brother. Paul found it hard as I looked into his eyes. He was struggling to keep it together. I simply said: "I love you…I'll be back soon." "I will be fine mum," I continued as I gave her a cuddle. "I love you all so much." As they wheeled me away I could hear them all crying. I just clutched dad's hand, ready to face it all over again.

I had kept my composure and all the way to the theatre – once again down the slope – I was still trying to crack jokes. "Now, madam," jested the anaesthetist, "it's time for the magic cream…and you want the epidural put in while you're asleep?" "Yes, please." I replied. "Oh…and the

catheter." Anything that could be done while I was asleep was a bonus in my eyes.

The banter was interrupted as Mr Cannon entered the small room outside the operating theatre. I tried to sneak a look inside the room itself, but I wasn't really sure whether I wanted to see it or not. Mr Cannon looked completely different out of his suit. He was gowned up, wearing gloves and a surgical mask and it kind of made me feel frightened. At that point, I looked in my dad's eyes and said: "I'm going to be fine dad…I love you." He kissed my forehead and I counted back from ten. I was asleep within a couple of seconds. Dad said later that as soon as I was asleep he was quickly pushed to one side and told to move away. Time was obviously of the essence and the less amount of time under anaesthetic the better. It took a few hours – but as I mentioned previously – I was the only one able to not think about it – I was out of it.

As I came round, for a split second I had forgotten what had just happened. All I was aware of was that I had had a deep sleep, no dreams, just a very, very deep sleep. That is, until I began to feel more awake, and as per usual I began shaking violently. They say it's a side effect of the

drugs in some cases – for me, it was something that always happened following surgery. In the recovery room I was wrapped in a blanket and all I can remember saying is: "Where is my family…do they know I'm okay?" But thoughts about others soon faded as I couldn't feel either of my legs, in fact, I couldn't feel anything below my waist and I was still shaking violently. It's hard to describe the actual feeling when you awake from an operation. I suppose that everyone's different. I felt as though I had a heavy object weighing down heavily on my body. I knew that the shakes would pass, but it was a horrible feeling and I wanted to fight it. From the second I could feel myself shaking I wanted to fight so that I would stabilise quicker and get back to the ward.

To be honest, the next couple of days were a blur. I had made it through the operation and was returned to the ward, but the amount of drugs I was taking plus the horrendous pain I was in meant that I slept with an oxygen mask on for most of the time. I do remember a couple of days after the operation having a terrible thirst. I was so desperately thirsty but I wasn't allowed to drink very much. Mum kept vigil by my bedside and stroked my

head while dad and Paul took it in turns to rub ice cubes over my lips. It wasn't long after that that I began to feel a tiny bit better. There was no cage over the stump this time. It was there for me to see. The outline was unmistakable and although because I still had the epidural in my back I couldn't actually feel anything, mentally I had a massive urge to bend my knee – which obviously was no longer there.

Over the following few days, while I spent most of my time asleep, my family took shifts to watch over me while I recovered. I had told them before I was admitted that I didn't want them to be tied to my bedside. I wanted them to get out and do things. I think it's probably depressing, exhausting and draining to sit in a hospital all day. Each day that passed I made a bit more progress. I was determined to get better and get home. I would try to push myself a little bit more each time, but to my horror, the pain I had prior to the operation was still very much there.

Then came the day that every amputee dreads – the arrival of the physiotherapists. It's the day that you're forced out of bed and the physiotherapist came early that

morning. Despite the fact that mentally I desperately wanted to get out and get on, I really didn't know how it would be possible, given the way I was feeling. My new stump felt heavy and I had a burning sensation which gave me the impression that the blood inside the stump was hot and trying to ooze out of the end of it. It sounds crazy, I know, but it's literally the only way I can describe it. I wanted to show the physiotherapist I was willing – that I was a fighter, but I did start by explaining the pain I was in. I wanted to be straight with her and I was hinting that I wanted her to be gentle with me.

My concerns obviously fell on deaf ears as she pulled back the bed sheets and said that we were going to get moving. As I lay on the bed I looked down at my new leg. The knee had gone and, yes, I did feel very much that a part of me had been taken away. I had a catheter still coming out from between my legs with a nearly full bag secured to the bed. The epidural was still in my spine to give pain relief and the last thing I felt like doing was getting out of bed. I appreciated that she was just doing her job and that I wasn't going to get out of it that easily.

From the moment we "got moving" it was painful. I

JUST A *Step*

had expected it to be, and I knew it wasn't going to be easy. But after lying in bed hooked up to machines and feeling pretty rough, it felt like an uphill struggle. She began by holding my arm and trying to get me to lean forward. She used her weight to get me lifted and all I could think about was what if these tubes come out? As I moved forward I gritted my teeth and pushed through the pain, determined to show that I was capable. All of sudden I'd made it. It probably sounds like such a minor thing, but at that moment, just that small amount of movement was an incredible achievement. "What we're going to try now," she started to explain, but I just couldn't believe my ears. Surely we're not going to do anything more? "No more!" I thought to myself but I was listening as she told me that she wanted to get me to the side of the bed.

I took a deep breath as she helped move my leg, but it felt so strange with still no real feeling in it and I was convinced that my muscles had deteriorated rapidly since I hadn't been using it for a while. We managed to get my right foot on the floor but by this time I was sweating profusely. I also felt as if I was about 90 years old. "Okay, Leanne," she continued, "we're now going to try and bring

around your stump." This was the part I was positively dreading. My stump was heavy and bandaged and the thought of someone touching it was unbearable. I had an incredible urge to protect it where I just wanted to hold it and not let anyone else close, but I could see that this lady meant business. It was probably the push that I needed however and as she wrapped her arms around my stump and prepared to move it she explained she would be counting to three. Every muscle in my body clenched. "You can do this," I told myself quickly trying not to squeal. "One…two…THREE", she lifted it firmly and tried to move it around to the side of the bed. She started muttering something but her voice was obliterated by the sound of me screaming. At that moment I didn't care who could hear me, or whether she thought I was being a baby. It was one of the worst pains I had ever experienced.

"Don't put it down…don't put it down!" I was screaming like a mad woman. Each time she tried to lower my stump I would shriek in agony – the pain was simply unbearable. I cried until I could cry no more and after around 30 minutes she was able to put my stump back in its original position. She told me to have a good rest and

that she would be back the next morning. Now there was something to look forward to! After she had gone I lay on the bed like a dead thing. I was absolutely exhausted. Who would have thought that doing something so simple would be so debilitating and I wondered if this recovery was going to take much longer than I had been hoping. By the time my family arrived for visiting they were quite shocked by my tear-stained face. They were pleased that I'd managed to move. I'd taken the first step – so to speak. The following day, Paul, Chris and Kate had to return home. There were work commitments to see to and I was glad that they'd be travelling together.

That evening, Chris stayed behind when the others left and we had one of the closest times we had ever experienced. He was a fantastic brother of whom I'd always felt protective. Perhaps he felt it was his turn to be protective of me. We talked about silly things and about great things we'd do when I was finally better. It was lovely to have that time with him and I greatly appreciated his gesture. He kissed me goodbye – which was a vulnerable thing for him to do. He always played the "tough guy" in everyday life and was probably too cool to kiss his big

sister, but that night he showed me his love and how he really felt. Early the next morning Paul came to visit before he set off for home. It was going to be hard to say goodbye, but I knew he'd be fine on his own. He'd lived on his own before I came along and was independent. I knew he'd look after himself and I was hoping he'd keep the house tidy! We talked for a while and then it was time for him to go. Watching the three of them go was difficult for me. I wasn't sure when I'd be seeing them again.

Mum and dad walked with them outside and while they were gone, Amy's mum came over to me with some fruit pastilles. It was kind of her and we hugged. I knew she'd been through a lot watching Amy being ill. I'd seen it in my own mum and in situations like this there are strong bonds – even if it is shown through a packet of sweets and a hug and the bonds I made with people will live with me forever. The next few days saw me get better and better. Progress was still slow and I didn't expect miracles, but gradually I could move slowly and it was an incredible achievement when I finally sat up in bed. Days were filled with visits from the physiotherapist, doctors' rounds and mum and dad sitting with me, stroking my

head and supporting me. Dad became a coach and each day would give me little goals to reach. It helped to make me stronger.

In the evenings, after mum and dad had left, was the time that I would relax and chill out. There were no physiotherapists to worry about and Evelyn, Amy and I would stay up late chatting and giggling. Even though Evelyn was a lot older than we twentysomethings, just like Marjorie, it didn't feel like it and we seemed to get on really well. I soon discovered that the remote control for the rented television at the bottom of my bed also controlled Evelyn's TV. I was a bit cheeky when she closed her eyes for a moment and I'd switch the channel and then giggle as she would open her eyes puzzled for a moment. It became the source of a lot of fun and it was the little things, like that, that helped pass the days away.

Then came a fantastic day when I finally managed to get out of bed. Coach dad, gave me the task of putting together a long list of all the things I would achieve. I now live by this every time I'm in hospital. For instance – having the epidural put in, getting through the operation, having the epidural removed. Having the catheter

removed. They were all things that had to be completed before I could go home. It was therapeutic being able to tick them off the list. Every time something was ticked off the list I was that little bit closer to making it home.

I'd managed, by now, not only to move around more and more, but I'd also managed to physically get out of bed and onto the chair beside it. It was the most amazing feeling and it was wonderful to have the sheets changed, my face washed and my hair thoroughly brushed. I even spent one evening sitting on the chair while I painted my nails. It was a fantastic feeling. It was difficult for me when Amy was ready to go home. She'd had part of her foot amputated and was ready to go and start preparing herself for her follow-up treatment. I was pleased for her, but selfishly didn't want her to leave. She'd become my friend and I was going to miss her and our midnight chats. Her family arrived to collect her and we hugged and exchanged numbers promising each other we'd keep in touch. I felt sad as I waved her goodbye and to be honest I was feeling a little bit jealous. Even though I knew she still had a long way to go and a massive battle ahead of her I was jealous that she was going home – right then, it

was my favourite place in the world.

More days drifted by and I became stronger and stronger. It was a huge milestone when I could finally get into a wheelchair and be taken to the physiotherapy department. When I was there I did a number of exercises and knew full well that if I was ever going to get home, the physiotherapists were the ones with a big say in the matter. I was out to impress. I still found things desperately hard though and the pain was immense. It even felt more painful than before the operation, but I put that down to post-operative pain and I thought it was probably normal at this stage in my recovery.

Evelyn was still opposite me and we had a lot of fun. Her family were great and I enjoyed seeing her sons and their families popping into visit. Somehow it reminded me of granny and maybe it was some kind of sign that we had met, just as I had felt it was with Marjorie. It was comforting to have someone around who was older – someone to make me laugh and see me through, just like granny would have done. After around 14 days – which by now had been feeling like a lifetime – I was allowed to go home. I went round kissing all the other patients goodbye

and had a great big hug with Evelyn. We also promised to stay in touch.

The journey home took about six hours in the back of an ambulance where I could feel every bump in the road. I had felt sick and was screaming in pain so it was huge relief when I finally made it to the front door. It was great seeing Paul again. I'd missed him and there was something about finally making it home that made me feel instantly better. Chris then announced that I was about to become an auntie! Kate and Chris told us that she was several weeks pregnant and my first thought was: "Oh, Chris…what have you done?" He was my little brother and I didn't even like to think he was having sex, never mind anything else and to be honest their news came as a big shock to the whole family. They hadn't been together that long and it was obviously a bolt from the blue. But, actually we all realised we were quite excited by the news. This was going to be great. So, we had lost something and now we were gaining something – all within a couple of weeks. You can't say that life was boring…

Back home I found I was more comfortable and, yes, the pain was still excruciating but each day I would have

lots of visitors, cards and letters. Charlie and Emma both came to see me regularly and the girls from work would come up and sit on the bed and have lunch. We gossiped and they gave me all the news which made me feel a part of it all again. While Paul was at work I was home on my own which gave me time to think my own thoughts and it gave me time to reflect on what I'd been through.

Everything had seemed to happen so fast and my life had been turned completely upside down. At that point, I hadn't had much time to sit back and think about very much and certainly not about what I'd been through. It gave me some comfort to think that maybe the fact I didn't manage to walk on the false limb before wasn't actually my fault after all. It was because all the while, I'd had this mass growing inside me. Although being ill again wasn't comforting, the fact that I wasn't to blame for the failed attempts with the false limb certainly was. Even though it was fantastic being back home and not cooped up in the hospital there were still little battles to face. There were the 60 or so stitches to be removed from my stump for a start. (I was a total baby the entire time it took for the stitches to come out and I screamed through the whole

procedure – mum was there to hold my hand.) I was also trying to wean myself off the drugs which was much easier said than done. I had been as high as a kite on morphine for some time and it was turning me into a zombie. But missing one dose would give me the sweats and shakes and there were hurdles over washing and going to the loo. I had managed to get upstairs which was one thing, but once up there I couldn't get down. I felt trapped upstairs. My bed had become my eating place, my meeting place, my washing place, my everything in fact and I soon got totally sick of looking at the same four walls. I'd have been better off in prison – at least I'd have been able to get about a bit – my bedroom became my prison. But another day was just around the corner that was going to change my life.

I was appointed a Macmillan nurse and she came to meet me. I had heard about Macmillan before and to be brutally honest I thought they only assigned you a nurse if you weren't going to get better and that they'd be there to try and make you more comfortable for your last few days. How wrong could I be?

My nurse was called Nicky and she was young, bubbly

and fun. Her help, turned out to be priceless. She would visit me regularly and monitor my progress. Nicky met my family and she gave them her number. She was also there to support them. I think it was a huge help for us all. Nicky was there for my family to talk to, as well as me, and she could understand their fears and worries and could answer the questions that any of us might have. She was a friend, a nurse and a fountain of knowledge all rolled into one and I'm so grateful to her that she was there. We'd sit down and I'd ask her silly questions – or I thought they sounded silly. However, she would listen, put my mind at rest and find out the answer if she needed to. Nothing was ever too much trouble and she looked after every part of me, whether it was trying to find a seat so I could sit in the bath, or to just be there and chat to me about random things. She was helping me find some sort of normality in my world that had just turned upside down.

It was by now a few weeks since my operation at Stanmore and, although the agony was still intense, I decided that enough was enough. I needed to wean myself off the morphine. At this time I was on so many drugs I didn't always know what day of the week it was and I felt

that losing my mind was "not me". I would rather put up with the pain. As I started to come off the morphine I suddenly developed withdrawal symptoms and one day in particular I suffered from diahorrea, sickness and hot and cold sweats. It was horrendous. I couldn't bear it and it took everything I had not to reach for the morphine bottle. But I couldn't give into the drug and I kept trying to tell myself that this was short-term hell for long term gain.

It was one of the worst days I had and before long I decided I had to ring Nicky. I felt awkward though. I was young and would get over this and I felt I might be taking her away from someone who needed her more than I did and it made me feel selfish, but I had no choice. I was desperate. I rang the number and cried down the phone. "I'm being dreadfully sick," I cried. "Please help me...I don't know what else to do." "Okay, Leanne...calm down and don't panic," she said in her gentle voice. "I'm going to get something and bring it round to you so sit tight and I won't be long." True to her word she was there on the doorstep, like an angel clutching a bag of anti-sickness pills. She was smiling. "Right," she said. "Let's get these

down you straight away and let's sort you out." Mentally, I think the fact she was there helped enormously and within a few minutes she'd managed to calm me down. She gave me a huge cuddle and if I'm honest, I wouldn't say my mask totally dropped when I was with Nicky, but I think she could see straight through it anyway, which was probably a good thing.

Once my brain was a little more my own and I was no longer on so many drugs, I found I could get up and start rebuilding my life once again. I was able to go back to the office, although to start with it was for short bursts only – it was hard to do much more and my colleagues would tell me off if they thought I'd spent too long there. That was one of the great things about sitting opposite my best friend and being surrounded by other friends. I couldn't get away with too much although I was pretty stubborn at times. But I gracefully accepted on some occasions that I literally couldn't do all the things that I'd done before. They were no longer possible.

As well as work I had a number of appointments to go to. There were visits to a physiotherapist in Camborne and trips back up to Derriford in Plymouth to try and get the

walking process started again. I was easily frustrated by the fact that my life had changed quite so much in just a few years. Where had my young, carefree life gone? The days of clubbing and drinking, flirting and not worrying about day-to-day things. My new world revolved around when was my next appointment? What tablets am I taking today? How can I get rid of this pain? When on earth will this nightmare be over?

I suppose you always get days when you feel a little more down than others, and I was luckily keeping my "down days" to myself. All the feelings and concerns that I had, I managed to hide from everyone. No one got to see the real me, although I did try to limit my self-pity at times. I decided to do something really positive and life-changing. Although the constant agony accompanied me everywhere, I went to the local BSM Driving School and queried how to get back my driving licence which had been taken away when I had my first amputation. I'm sure the ladies in the office thought I was mad. I'd "driven" my wheelchair into the office – how could I even think about driving a car? But, I had fire in my belly and I was determined. I had to apply to DVLA and fill in a huge

number of medical forms. Luckily I had lost my left leg so having the right one still intact meant I could still drive an automatic. "Every cloud…" I told myself.

There were a few anxious weeks of waiting before I received the response I wanted. DVLA confirmed that it was okay for me to regain my licence although I would have to take a driving test first. "Easier said than done!" I thought as it was some time since I had last driven. It seemed as if it would be even tougher now, plus I had to take the theory test. I actually felt quite old sitting in the examination room and I felt even more under pressure because Kate was taking her test at the same time. I didn't want to fail and look an idiot, but I didn't want to pass if she failed. Luckily we both passed with flying colours. She wanted to take her test before the baby was born and I wanted to take the test as for me, it meant FREEDOM.

Over the next few weeks I had driving lessons – just another thing to add to the various other appointments happening at the time, but I knew it would be worth it in the end. Or, I certainly hoped that it would as I had so much pain in my stump it was hard to concentrate. I was meanwhile getting concerned as to why the pain was still

so bad. After a day of work, an evening of driving and 24 hours full of pain I came home and decided to give Amy and Evelyn a call. I was so pleased that we had all kept in touch, which personally for me, I found a massive help and support.

In the first few days that I was recovering at home I would spend ages on the phone to Amy. Both of us would be watching *This Morning* or *Loose Women* which was on in the background as we'd compare how our scars were doing, announcing when our stitches were out and I think, just generally being there for each other. I was looking forward to phoning Amy that night and catching up on all the latest. I also wanted to tell her that I was learning to drive again and that I would soon be an auntie.

I was a bit surprised when Amy didn't answer the phone. Instead, Jay, her boyfriend – who I'd met at Stanmore – was on the other end of the line. "Hi, Jay," I said cheerily, "how's everything going? Hope you're all well?" I could tell something was wrong immediately when he replied by the tone in his voice. "I've been meaning to call, Leanne", he started. "Amy's not very well." My heart dropped like a stone. "What can I do?" I asked

immediately, always believing I could do something to help. "Thank you" came his response "But there's nothing you can do…she's been moved into a hospice and she's very poorly…I'll pass on your love." I could tell he was struggling to speak and I sent all my love and I told him he knew where I was if they needed anything.

As I dropped the phone I felt a desperate sadness. I felt helpless that I couldn't do anything and I felt sorrow thinking of what they were all going through. I suppose I was even reflective – thinking about what it would be like if I had been in that situation. For the next few days my mind was consumed with Amy and her family and what they were all going through. I was confident that she was just going through a bad patch and she'd soon turn it around. She was a strong character and I knew she was a fighter. Also she was young and I knew that went in her favour. I continued with my own life, but she was never far from my mind, but I tried not to let it get me down – I wanted to stay positive.

I hadn't told anyone in my family that I was planning to take a driving test, but I had told them and the girls at work that I was taking a few "refresher" lessons, which I

suppose was partly true. My driving instructor, Kevin, was great and he helped give me bags of confidence. He also had a really calming effect and he was aware just how important it was to me that I pass my test. When the day of the test arrived in early January, he was right behind me, supporting me all the way. I was really nervous on the morning of the test and, apart from the theory, I hadn't had a test or sat an exam for ages. Bearing in mind that it took me three attempts the first time round I was feeling pretty petrified.

I left the house that morning telling Paul I was just going to have another lesson. I thought that if I told him the truth I would only be putting more pressure on myself and there would be people to tell if I failed. Over the next two hours I felt like jelly, my knees – well knee – was knocking and I couldn't believe how nervous I was. I think it was because it was much more than a driving test to me. It was the key to freedom and it would be something really positive that I would have achieved on my own. I was really worried that the examiner would take one look at me and think I would be no good behind the wheel because I only had one leg. On the other hand I didn't want sympathy

and I wanted to do my best and for that to be the only thing that would be judged.

As I walked, on my crutches, into the test centre waiting room I felt the eyes of everyone else there waiting to be tested upon me. It was a regular, if not daily occurrence. I was used to stares, glances, looks, glimpses, peeks – you name it, I had had it and I suppose over time I got used to it. I was fine with the way I looked now and so were the people that mattered around me. The examiner entered the room and called my name. I followed him out to the car and my heart was racing. After 40 minutes of parallel parking, emergency stopping and mirror, signal, manoeuvre we returned to the centre and he asked me to stop the engine. I also had to remove my seatbelt. I could feel the sweat on my palms as I awaited my fate.

"Leanne, I'm pleased to tell you that you've passed with flying colours!" he said with a smile. I didn't know what to do with myself, I felt as though I was going to burst with excitement. I felt so proud of myself that I had come through such a terrible time and I had managed to achieve something so positive. Once out of the car I

hugged Kevin and as we drove back to Truro tears of joy rolled down my cheeks. For once they weren't tears of sadness.

I was like the "cat that got the cream" when I went home and told my family and friends what I'd done. Paul and I immediately went out to buy a car. "I deserve it!" I thought to myself as I sat behind the wheel of my new Picasso. It was one of the best things I had ever owned and the feeling of being outside, driving around on my own was priceless. Much like the electric wheelchair, this too enabled me to have more independence and it was just one step closer to the life I had once had. Although I was over the moon with my new car and spent every free moment driving around, catching up with friends, driving along the coast and feeling young again with the radio blasting out my favourite songs, I couldn't forget about Amy. I hadn't heard for a few days how she was and I just kept hoping that she was too busy with her family to have time to ring me back.

On a rare day when I wasn't in my new car, I was out shopping in my wheelchair when my mobile phone rang. The number on the display said "Amy" so I quickly pulled

into an aisle of coats so I wouldn't be in anyone's way. I was surprised when it was Jay on the other end. "Hi, Jay…is everything alright?" I asked concerned. "Hi, Leanne," he said. "I just called to let you know that Amy died yesterday." I felt sick and I just couldn't take in what I was hearing. She was young, she had been strong. How could this have happened? In truth, the rest of that day was a blur. I felt helpless. My heart went out to her family. I was wondering what her mum was going through and I was asking myself how they were even coping.

It was unimaginable and I think I felt slightly guilty. Guilty that I was still here, living, breathing and able to laugh with my friends, for passing my driving test – for god's sake – when she was going through all of that. It was just so unfair. I spent a long period of time questioning everything. I couldn't help it and it's hard not to compare something like that to your own situation. It made it all the more real and I realised that no one was invincible and that the worst could happen to anyone at anytime. All I could hope was that she was somewhere beautiful and no longer in pain. Although I hadn't known her for very long, she was someone I had met along my own painful journey

and she was someone I would never forget. The news also hit my family and friends hard. I think they could all imagine what Amy's family and friends were going through and once again, the enormity of it all truly hit home.

I was also worried because I couldn't get hold of Evelyn. The last news I'd had was that she too had been moved to a hospice, in Bushey, near London. I had no idea which hospice and one evening I spent over an hour trying to track her down. I wanted to find her to put my mind at rest, but I didn't get anywhere. I just wanted to hear her voice and I knew she would understand how I was feeling about Amy. The fact I couldn't get hold of her was a real worry and there was nothing I could do. I filled my time and tried really hard not to dwell on the recent sad events so I threw myself into everything. I still had the regular meetings with Nicky, my Macmillan nurse, and work was busy, so it was extremely good for me. The pain in my stump still hadn't subsided so I was now being treated by a pain team at the Royal Cornwall Hospital as an outpatient. I was trying everything I could to get myself better.

The appointments at the Derriford limb clinic still weren't going so well which was much to my disappointment. I know in light of recent events it might seem trivial, but it was a big thing for me and I was extremely frustrated. I had now spent a long time getting around on crutches and my arms ached and the lack of mobility was having a huge impact on my life. Things that people take for granted were things that I desperately missed. I hadn't been able to have a shower in more than two years – don't worry, I could get in the bath – but it was an effort lifting my body in and out of it and a shower was something I craved. I knew that if I never walked again my arms wouldn't last forever and underneath I was really worried about it. I'd spoken to my consultant at the limb centre and he was as baffled as me as to why I still wasn't walking. It now felt as though I would never walk again and perhaps I needed to start thinking about my future. I discussed my concerns with Nicky on one of her visits and told her that I was worried that if I didn't walk again then my body would deteriorate and that even though I was only in my twenties I was beginning to get very tired.

I talked to Paul that evening and decided that I should

plan for the future and that if I needed something I would go out and get it. We decided that we would have a downstairs toilet and shower built which would make a world of difference for me. Apart from the fact that I still had a hideous commode sitting in the corner of the living room – it was practical, but rather depressing – at least if the building work was carried out I could at last have a shower. In the coming weeks we met a builder, got some plans drawn up and sent it out for tender. I was really excited and hoped the work would start soon. After all, how much could a simple downstairs toilet and shower room cost? The question was soon answered as the responses from builders began to come through the post.

"Nearly £25,000?" I shrieked to Paul – and that was the lowest quote. "How on earth are we going to find that kind of money?" I asked, as my heart fell to the floor as my dreams of washing my hair, sitting in a lovely new easy to access shower faded. "We'll find it," Paul replied. He was trying to reassure me, but the truth was that we simply didn't have that kind of money. During the past couple of years, being poorly had meant that I had to spend a lot of money on prescriptions and therapies and I think most people of

my age wouldn't have that kind of money stashed in the bank. I hated asking for help, but I felt I had no choice other than to speak to social services. Me being able to take a shower was, at that time, more important than my pride.

I made an initial call, expecting to start the ball rolling and to gain lots of helpful advice. But instead, the lady assigned to me was not helpful at all. She listened to my story and understood my need, but when it came to receiving possible help it was a case of: "Well, you work, so you aren't entitled to any financial support." I was gobsmacked. I had never really asked for anything before and assumed that as I had paid my National Insurance since starting work that I would be entitled to some help when I really needed it the most. I was wrong. I wasn't even given any advice about where I might go, or people to ring who might possibly have helped me. The only thing she mentioned was that maybe if I didn't work then I might be entitled to some kind of financial assistance. It was something to think about for the future. This, I have to say, enraged me. The fact that I was being penalised for working made me feel sick. The whole time throughout my illness I'd dragged my backside into work, I'd always

worked hard and I didn't just want to be another unemployment statistic. That wasn't me. That would never be me – I just wasn't raised that way. I decided then and there that I would not give up my job and I would raise the money myself.

When I called the office back the following day I explained what I intended to do. I was still looking for some sort of support – even if it was just to back my decision – but again I was shocked with the woman on the other end of the phone. "You're going to raise £25,000 yourself?" she chuckled down the phone. I felt she was mocking me cruelly and unnecessarily. "I think you're being rather optimistic," she said. "I like a challenge," I responded rather promptly before saying goodbye and hanging up the phone.

I hadn't wanted to be rude – no matter how rude she had just been to me. I was brought up to respect people, no matter how tough that was at times – and in a strange way I had a lot to thank her for. She had just made more me determined than ever to prove her wrong. Now, I know £25,000 is a massive amount to raise, and if I was honest I didn't know where to start, but I reasoned I had got through a great deal worse and so this wasn't going to beat me either.

I knew I needed to aim big. If I'd opted to do car boot sales, sponsored walks and raffles we'd have been raising the money forever. Also, coming from a proud family, I was aware of the fact that I didn't want to "ask" people for money. I had always worked for what I had and I'd always been financially independent and I had the same attitude to this project too. I wasn't a charity case and it wasn't up to others to bail me out. I started off thinking there must be some kind of help for people in my position. We do live in a very fortunate country and there must be thousands of people in similar situations, just needing a little help at a time of need. I contacted everyone I could think of: Comic Relief, The National Lottery…but every morning I opened the post was to face another rejection letter.

Dear Miss Grose

Unfortunately, as you are not a registered charity you would not be eligible for any funding.

Dear Miss Grose

It is with regret that on this occasion we are unable to help you.

LEANNE GROSE

The letters went on and on and at first it was very demoralising. Apart from actually winning the lottery, the chances of me getting this bathroom seemed more and more remote. It wasn't even as if I were asking for a little help for something extravagant, like a swimming pool in the back garden, new car...cuddly toy! It was a necessity and what I believed to be a basic human right to be able to wash with ease and to actually go to the loo in a bathroom and not have to ask any visitors to go outside when I needed a pee in the living room commode – it was humiliating. So that was the first avenue exhausted. I now knew that as I wasn't a registered charity that I wouldn't get any help from a lot of big organisations so the next natural question was, could I register as a charity? NO, was the answer I gave myself. I couldn't do it. It would feel selfish and that just wasn't me, no matter how badly I wanted a shower. At least I knew where I stood, but instead of giving up I decided to try another hairbrained idea.

I didn't want to ask for money, but I obviously needed some, so I decided to think like a business. I wasn't a charity; I didn't even like the sound of the word in my case so I thought I would run an event. Not just any old event,

it would have to be something on a massive scale which would generate a great deal of income and that people would be desperate to attend. I wanted to provide a service to the public that meant that although it would mean a lot of hard work I would be able to sleep at night knowing that I had achieved something in the best possible way. I could then keep my head held high and not be thought of as a charity case. I also wanted to wipe the smile from the social worker's face! Isn't it strange how sometimes when people imply you can't do something it really gives you the drive, energy and determination to prove them wrong? That was what I desperately wanted to do.

The first event I thought of was a girl's night in. I knew that everyone loved Body Shop and Virgin Vie parties. I wanted to plan one massive girly night. There were so many things to organise and I wanted to get on with it as soon as possible. It was going to be tough though. I was still in a lot of pain and of course there was the mobility issue – racing around on a pair of sticks wasn't that practical plus I was back working full time. It was certainly not going to be easy. I booked a day off work and sat down to plan my event from scratch.

LEANNE GROSE

I loved programmes like *The Apprentice* and *Dragon's Den* and thrived on adrenaline. I realised it would be stressful, but I also thought it would be a very interesting ride. My priority was the venue. I spoke to a wonderful lady called Kelly from the Alverton Manor Hotel in Truro. The Alverton is a high-class hotel and had a certain something about it which would give the night an air of exclusivity and credibility. It also had beautiful rooms which would have been ideal and I didn't want women arriving at a social club or pub. The whole night needed to be centred around extravagance and luxury. And, not only did I want to raise money from this, I wanted to provide a fantastic night out where women would have a great time. It suddenly wasn't just about raising money.

I was overwhelmed when the Alverton Manor agreed to host my event for free. At first it had been hard asking people to help me out with that sort of thing, but my confidence grew as the prospect of sitting on that plastic commode in the living room for the foreseeable future was far more degrading for me. That thought definitely spurred me on. The whole way along I tried to think with my business head on and I knew it was rare to get

something for nothing in this world so I began using other tools at my disposal.

I contacted the local newspapers and radio stations to advertise my event. I knew it would be fantastic publicity plus it would highlight the problem with the systems in place – for people in my situation – and I wanted to show that you can do *anything* if you put your mind to it. I wasn't used to the media – I was around six years old when I once spoke on the radio. I was supposed to be speaking about a local farm, but it was a disaster when I froze as the microphone came anywhere near me. But, this was different. I had grown up and the past couple of years had shown me that I was strong and that deep down, somewhere inside me, I could fight on and do anything. But, the responses I received would leave me staggered.

As soon as I went public, everyone wanted my story. I was anxious to point out that it wasn't a sob story – I was a happy and lucky young woman who was putting on an event to raise funds for a downstairs loo and shower room. I desperately didn't want people to feel sorry for me. As well as organising the event, plus all my other commitments, weekends were filled with radio interviews,

newspaper articles and photo shoots all drumming up as much attention as possible in order to sell tickets for my big "Girls' Night In". I soon found that people were amazing – word had spread that this event was taking place and we received requests for tickets before they were even printed. I had managed to secure the services of a lady who was an expert in fashion and beauty – a Cornish version of Trinny, or Susannah, if you like, and she had agreed to come along and give a talk. I had also managed to find a very sexy young musician, called Tony, who said he would come and entertain while also working as compere for the evening. I just knew he would go down well with the ladies.

I then really struck gold when several local businesses stepped up and said that they too wanted to help out. Next, Monsoon, Accessorize, the Body Shop and Lush all wanted to be part of my "Girls' Night In". The response was simply overwhelming and I felt incredibly humbled that so many people and businesses wanted to help to make the night a success. I had a list of things to do as long as my arm – the tickets were printed, posters were put up in local shops and those who had offered to help

me even sold tickets in their stores. Each ticket cost £25.00 which I worried about at first and I had exactly 100 to sell. But, before I knew it, within days, the tickets were sold out! The pressure was now really on to make this night lavish and magical.

Every weekend leading up to the big event I was racing around in my car, collecting raffle prizes and doing last minute jobs. I also spent some money on lots of handmade chocolates while I tried desperately to cover all bases. The other thing women love are flowers and the amazing ladies at the Garden Centre in Tresillian just outside Truro offered to come along and show how to make hanging baskets and to sell flowers. Then there was pampering. I had nail technicians, hairdressers and make-up artists all booked for the evening to help the ladies that attended feel like "a million dollars". I had also managed to hire – at a good rate – some musical entertainment, but even with the amount going on I still wanted that little bit extra to make it all the more special. My main priority was no longer about money. Now it was about giving 100 women one of the best nights of their lives and so I came up with another grand idea.

I decided to put on a fashion show with the help of the kind people at the stores who had offered to help. We were almost there! One of my bosses had a beautiful daughter, called Katie, who rallied up all her school friends and they were all incredibly excited about being the models. They were all a bit nervous though as none of them had done it before, but they soon got into the swing of it when we practised and the music was pumping. I had even managed to borrow some staging from a local school – London Fashion Week; eat your heart out! After weeks of planning, publicising, negotiating and racing around, the day had finally arrived. I had booked the day off work and dad came over to the Alverton Manor early to help me set everything up. There was so much to do – I'd spent the night before writing lists with military precision to ensure that everything would go exactly as planned. But, when dad and I arrived at the Alverton my jaw could have hit the floor. It looked absolutely amazing. Lavish red velvet curtains hung elegantly and complimented the red and gold velvet chairs – the Alverton had originally been a convent and we were holding the event in what was once the Chapel. Perhaps fitting for a girls' night in – although

I doubt the former Sisters of the Epiphany had seen anything like it. When I worked it out, I had spent a lot of money organising the event because I had wanted it to be special and to be of a high standard. It was a risky gamble.

It wasn't long before the hall was a hive of activity, the girls came to practice their technique on the catwalk and volunteers were putting up the staging while others were putting out chairs positioned carefully along the fashion runway. Dad and I raced out to collect some last minute bits. Gifts for the girls to say "thank you", trays of food that had been kindly donated by a catering company – oh, the list was endless. I could probably have paid for the extension with the amount I was clocking up on my mobile phone that was constantly glued to my ear. I felt like a high-flying business woman working on the London Stock Market or something: "Buy, sell, buy!" If I didn't have organisational skills beforehand, I certainly did by then. By the end of the day I was absolutely exhausted and my stump was shaking with pain. It was one of those times when I was being reminded that I wasn't the same as every other twentysomething and I just physically couldn't do anymore.

Paul, mum, dad, Chris and Kate all told me to go home and get ready – everything would be fine they reassured me. I had done as much as I could and it was just a few last minute bits and pieces that needed to be finished so I reluctantly went home on my own to get ready. As soon as I got through the front door I felt like I could have cried. I was so very tired and I knew that nothing, other than sleep, would fix it. I had a nice relaxing bath and spent the next hour getting "dolled-up" for my big night. Then it was time to head back to the Alverton where I was hoping against hope that the gamble would pay off and that the evening would be a success.

As I walked through the doors my eyes filled with tears – the room looked absolutely spectacular. Everyone that had promised to come along and help was there working away and I was blown away by the fact they had all come for me. They were there to help me and I was completely overwhelmed. The catwalk came right down the middle of the room and all the way along there were beautiful balloons in pink and purple – feminine, I thought. Along the back were the lovely ladies from Tresillian Garden

Centre who had definitely gone all out. They were setting up an amazing table filled with plants and flowers for sale and two of these ladies were even sorting out the raffle tickets for me – they were fabulous.

At the other end of the room, it looked like some high class London-style pampering parlour with gorgeous smelling products, bowls for women to have treatments, hairstylists ready and waiting with their straighteners and a gorgeous male nail technician who had agreed to help out at the very last minute. On each chair for each lady there were two goody bags. One was from Lush while the other was from the Body Shop – both contained some wonderful free products – it was simply all amazing. As the guests started to arrive I could see by their faces that they hadn't been expecting quite such lavishness. They knew they were in for a treat.

I "worked" the room, making sure that everyone was happy and had what they needed. I also checked that all those helping out were okay and whether anyone needed anything. I then gave a pep talk to the now nervous, but still excited, girls next door who were busy getting changed for their big fashion show. Photographers had

arrived from across the county and I felt like a real somebody as I was asked to pose for pictures and give interviews. Several times, through the throng of women everywhere, I would catch a glimpse of my family who spent the evening winking at me. They were letting me know that it was a success and that they were there for me. As the evening was girls only, obviously Paul, dad and Chris strictly shouldn't have been there so I had come up with the idea that they should be dressed in tuxedoes so that they could act as waiters for the evening. They strutted through the crowds serving ladies with canapés, chocolates and strawberries – they loved every second of it. I was particularly proud to see my dad loving his new job. He was quite shy and I wasn't sure what he'd make of the situation, but he was in his element and some ladies were even pinching their bottoms as they walked past. The three of them looked like characters out of a James Bond movie and they became my superheroes. The ladies took their seats around the catwalk and the evening officially began. Tony, the compere, worked his magic with the microphone and definitely geed up the crowd. There was an incredible buzz in the room and Paul's mum Trina, who

was dressed to the nines, was having a whale of a time with her friends. It was just fabulous.

We started the evening with an auction which reminded me why I was trying to raise money out of the event – which was something that had reached the back of my mind with all the excitement and hysteria surrounding me. That's when I met Philip Buddell, a local auctioneer who had volunteered his services through a mutual friend at work. He was a tall, strong-looking man who with his deep rich voice could have commanded any audience. He certainly managed it with the ladies who were soon eating out of the palm of his hand. I was fascinated listening to him and was relieved to find that the auction was not going to be the "boring" bit, which I had certainly thought it might be. Philip made the auction an amazing feature of the evening and the magnificent prizes I'd managed to secure from local companies were going down a storm. I had approached companies asking for something that could be sold, rather than money, and for something that would promote their businesses. I had been given Toni & Guy vouchers, a dozen oysters with champagne, gorgeous jewellery and there was even a

voucher for someone to have their oven cleaned. The women went wild. Wine flowed and the bids started thick and fast. It was all quite overwhelming and when the auction was over I hurried next door to see how the girls were getting on with their changing. They were virtually ready for their big entrance.

The room was pumping as the music began which I'd specifically chosen for a "girl" theme. Each song was certainly toe-tapping and there was something for every generation from "Girls Just Want To Have Fun" to "Material Girl". The starlets were ready. I moved to the back of the room where I could just take it all in as the fashion show began. I knew my smile was huge as all the young girls gave the catwalk 100 percent. They were stunning and I felt extremely proud of them all. There were several changes and they modelled "going out" styles and "casual" to "dressy eveningwear" but nothing prepared me for the finale. I had rehearsed and practised the final walk with the models so I thought I knew what I was about to see. The final song, "It's Raining Men" by the Weather Girls, was one of my all time favourites and the girls literally galloped down the catwalk in front of three

new models – Paul, dad and Chris!

They were all dressed in outfits provided by the stores involved and they looked incredible. They all carried flowers in their arms and began throwing them out to the, by now, baying hordes of women who were going absolutely wild. I had tears in my eyes looking at them up on the catwalk, giving it their all, and still loving every single minute. Women were wolf-whistling, and each of the three men in my life seemed to have taken on a completely different persona. My usually shy dad was dancing and laughing, Paul did a moonwalk to screams from the audience and the proud feelings I had watching them were almost overwhelming. It was a fantastic end to what had been a real night to remember. Women were grabbing me, hugging me and kissing me. They were wishing me all the luck in my efforts to raise the money I needed and I felt that something amazing had happened. Profits aside, I felt I had made some new friends. Friends who had selflessly done all of this for me and I'd never forget their kindness and generosity. Although it was fabulous it was also an exhausting day and as a large group of us stayed to tidy up all I could think about was my bed.

I kissed all the beautiful Tresillian ladies goodbye. They'd spent the entire evening making up bouquets while the wonderful staff from Lush and the Body Shop had gone above and beyond anything I'd expected. Then there were my catwalk beauties, Philip, and my family. The list of people I had to thank was endless and I felt incredibly humble. Although I felt like a zombie, I was still on a tremendous high as we arrived home. Mum and dad had come home with Paul and me and we decided to see if we'd made a profit.

Before there was time to count it I told the three of them that whatever money was there it didn't matter. I'd had such a wonderful night – even if it was slightly stressful and I was extremely tired. I felt as though I'd met some of the best people I could possibly have met and then we counted the money. We were all gobsmacked. In one night there was a profit of more than £3,000. Despite being tired I found it incredible that one night had produced that much profit. As my head hit the pillow I was wondering what my next big project might be.

The event really knocked the stuffing out of me but it also made me even more determined. I knew now that I

could raise the money and, although there was still a huge mountain to climb, I knew I couldn't do six or seven girls' nights, so I decided I would need to focus all my attention on one huge, mind-blowing event, one which could raise the money we needed to fulfil my dream of having that all-important downstairs bathroom – and my independence. While I was deciding what to do next, I began receiving letters of support from people who had read about me in the newspapers or who had heard me bleating about my cause on the radio. I think many people got behind me because I was fighting for something. I didn't sit on my backside and complain – I didn't think "poor me" – there were no stories of me pleading poverty or asking for sympathy. I used the publicity for the right reasons and I think, well, I hoped, that that's how other people saw it too.

The pain was still very much there and my appointments to the pain clinic and by now to a special consultant in Oncology were even more frequent. Hospital had become a massive part of my life and unfortunately I had to accept it. While friends were out partying and doing everything that girls my age would do, I would

spend some evenings crawling up the stairs, tears pouring down my face. I was tired, in desperate pain, but nobody saw that. It was my own secret world and I didn't, I suppose, really show anyone just how tough it actually could be a great deal of the time. The friends from school were still a part of my life. Donna had been good at staying in touch and would often phone me to see if I was okay. Chantelle was great at coming to the hospital with me and keeping me cheered while I waited. Lisa, Kay, Kelly, Vicky and Laura were also still around for me and we had kept in touch to a point. We didn't speak every day but I felt I still had friends and we'd make a special point of meeting up at Christmas.

But things had changed though. Maybe I was being paranoid, but I suppose there were some elements to our lives now which meant that we had drifted apart and each of us had different priorities. I suppose I also felt like a bit of a burden. I couldn't go clubbing – well, actually I could have done, but I felt that I would have held them up or cramped their style. I used to be the life and soul when we were all younger, but now I felt a little redundant. The calls were becoming less and less from each of them and I

tended to only see any of them if I was in hospital. Maybe it was paranoia but they made me feel that I was not really included anymore. It was definitely different and whereas I had thought I had a good number of friends, it was slowly becoming apparent to me that the word "friend" was something quite special and included people that stuck with you through thick and thin.

When I thought about how close I was to Charlie and Emma, Nathan and my new friends, Christine and Forest, I realised just how much things had changed from school days. Charlie and Emma and the ever-gorgeous Nathan knew me inside out and upside down. It was the little things they knew about me. Charlie would always know if my pain was particularly bad – even though I tried to hide it – in fact, all the girls at work seemed to know – they had it down to a fine art and I was finding it increasingly difficult to conceal when I was in pain.

My work colleagues were particularly excited about the fundraising. Rachael, who was always super organised and efficient offered to help in anyway she could and it wasn't long before the whole of Carrick were behind me. It meant a great deal. Mum's work colleagues at the Manor House

Dental Practice in St Austell had rallied together and kindly organised a sponsored walk. The momentum was really growing and we were all working together as a team to hit the target.

Then one day, the perfect idea for my next event popped into my head. But it wasn't going to be easy. In fact it was going to be a mammoth task, but I wanted to aim high. "The bigger the risk, the bigger the reward!" I told myself, knowing that if I could pull it off then it would be the end of my worries. I made some calls and made copious notes about ideas and my head was literally buzzing with thoughts. I was excited and wanted to tell the whole world my idea. I sat my family down and pitched the idea to them. They had proved an invaluable test audience in the past. "I've had an idea," I said as I looked at all their faces which were basically saying: "Oh, no – what now?" "Where is the biggest and one of the most spectacular places I could hold an event?" I continued. I could see they were racking their brains and as no one could give me an answer I was bursting to tell them: "The Eden Project!" I blurted. The instant smiles told me I had actually come up with something good. As one of the

modern wonders of the world, the Eden Project was built in a disused clay pit and boasted amazing biomes, beautiful plants and flowers and was truly something phenomenal.

I had no idea whether it was even possible to hire Eden, but I knew that if it was, then my event could be risky, but positively huge.

Chapter 7

Blag it

I was soon in full flow with planning and getting useful numbers for contacts I had formed. It was going to work in a very similar way to the girls' night, and I wanted to once again use the press and media to gain good coverage as a big incentive to persuade businesses to help. I needed excellent publicity but I was already aware that I needed to think on a much larger scale than before. The first and most obvious task was to approach Eden itself. Initially when I had mentioned my plan to people some had laughed and said it would never happen while others started guessing how much it would all cost. One person mentioned that they'd heard it cost £15,000 to hire the venue. This didn't frighten me or put me off, it simply excited me. I was aware of how great it would be if I could pull it all off.

I arranged a meeting with the creator of the Eden Project's second in command, Jo Gale. I prepared myself

for the meeting and was suited and booted with my proposal in place for what I needed from them. I was desperately hoping that my dream could become a reality. As soon as I entered the offices at Eden I felt at ease. The staff were so friendly and kind to me and it generally felt like a nice place to be. It was obvious that everyone who worked there had a real passion for Eden and all that it stood for. I met with the lady responsible for event management who worked closely with Jo. I began to get a little more nervous as the more I looked around the more I wanted to hold my event there. The more potential I saw, the more I could envisage people having an amazing night out.

As we started the meeting I put forward my proposal and of course the conversation turned to money. It would cost far more than I could afford to hire the Eden Project as it was extremely expensive, but after more discussion, it was announced that I could have the venue for my event for free. I just couldn't believe it. As I tried to remain calm and play it cool, my tummy was doing somersaults and I was so excited that I wanted to burst. Friends and family just couldn't believe the deal I'd struck either and I felt

incredibly proud. So now I had the venue, but I still had so much to do. I decided to look at the overall theme as I felt this would be a good place to start planning my ideas. I wanted something very professional and I didn't want just an average night out in Cornwall. It had to be extremely enticing so that people would want to buy tickets.

I decided to name the event "Leanne's Summer Ball" and it was to be a black tie event where women could dress up and it would provide all those who wanted to come with the chance to have a mad night out. I personally felt that a more formal approach would give the evening some style and would allow it to be just as lavish as the girls' night in but on a much larger scale. Riding on the success of securing the venue, I knew I had to pull out all the stops to make it more than a fundraiser. I wanted it to be a night that everyone would remember. It felt like a task for the television programme *The Apprentice*.

So, here I was, a young, one-legged girl who had worked in the same job practically since leaving school, who was now trying to arrange the ball of the century. I was learning on the job – sales, marketing,

communication, finances and budgeting. You name it, I learnt about it and I felt that the exercise was making me stronger day by day as I met new people, achieved new things and each day took one step closer to achieving my dream. I had a whopping 1,000 tickets to sell and the thought of shifting just 100 felt daunting enough. I wanted to make sure, as I had done previously, that people got great value for their money, so tickets were priced at £25.00 each. I was still a little worried, I suppose, that maybe it was slightly too expensive, but I was determined, again, as before, that it would be an amazing night out.

A great deal of time was spent thinking about catering. It was important. What about a buffet? That would be considerably cheaper than a sit-down meal. Then I stopped myself. I wasn't going to compromise the evening with a few sausages on sticks and a selection of dips. If the evening was to be a huge success I would have to go all out and take a massive gamble. After lengthy discussions with Eden with regard to the food, I bit the bullet and ordered a meal. They would provide different dishes of Thai Green curry, pastas and potato dishes. It would be a three-course meal with something for everyone. Of course,

a top meal was going to mean that it would eat heavily into any profit, but it was a gamble I knew I should take. The more things I planned for the evening, the more the whole project grew and grew. I put tickets on sale in Ottakar's Bookshop and the Body Shop, Lush, Next and Monsoon all agreed, once again, to sell them for me. Other people also kindly offered to sell them as I realised that this was a much larger project and it would take a great deal of effort to shift enough tickets to just break even. Then I had a brainwave!

As this was to be a unique evening where businesses and business people would be coming along – hopefully to spend some money and enjoy a night out, I wondered if I could get sponsorship for the event. As with the idea of using the media, I knew sponsorship would be a great way to promote a local business and it would give me the financial advantage to make it a truly mind-blowing event. I started writing letters to as many businesses as possible but the responses were disappointing and they were always the same. As I wasn't a registered charity it made it difficult for companies to fully support the event. Still determined not to be beaten or get downhearted I ploughed on

thinking of other ways I could get a sponsor. Then it struck me. Who had a massive company in Cornwall and actually lived in the county? I had someone in mind and did a bit of digging until I found out roughly where he lived.

His name was Tony and I knew he was a millionaire with a lot of businesses as well as a great deal of power. Later that day with a fresh idea in my mind I decided to drive down to the area in which he lived. As I arrived I had no clue which house it was or even if I was in the right location so I decided to go to the biggest house I could find. It had large wooden electric gates and looked extremely grand. Luckily the gates were open as there was a lot of work being carried out at the time. Without even thinking I drove through the gates with my heart racing. The workmen stopped and came over and by now I was actually really scared. I decided to "blag it" and tried to stay calm.

"Hi," I said, trying not to show any sign that I had absolutely no idea where I was. "Is Tony in?" I continued casually as if he were my friend. My back up plan, should I be in the wrong place, was to say: "Oh, sorry, he must have moved," or "I've got the wrong house, obviously," but

I was gobsmacked when the response came. "No, love…I'm afraid he's not in today… He's at meetings or something. He drove off this morning, but I assume he'll be back tonight though." "Thank you…I'll give him a shout later," I said, trying hard to contain the smile that was threatening to erupt all over my face. The adrenaline that was pumping through my body made me think I was about to explode. I waved goodbye to the unsuspecting workmen who had kindly let me know I'd struck the jackpot. It had been pure luck that my instincts had taken me to the right house.

I raced home to talk to Paul, who by now was more and more surprised with the news I was giving him each day. He said I'd done a great job with the event already, but I wondered deep down if he actually thought I could raise the money we needed. That afternoon I concentrated on one or two other things, made some more calls, booked some more acts for the evening and all the while tried to gather the confidence I needed to go back to the millionaire's house whom I was hoping would help me.

As I drove back later that evening to the house where he lived my stomach was gurgling as I began to get more

than a little bit nervous. I mean, it was probably a crazy thing to do, but I felt it was the only thing I could do and apart from some possible embarrassment I had nothing to lose. As I pulled up outside, my heart sank as the open giant wooden gates were now closed. "That's it!" I told myself – resigned to the fact that it obviously wasn't meant to be. I turned the key in the ignition and as I did so I saw car lights in my rear view mirror. It was coming towards me and as it passed me the entry gates opened wide and the car drove in. Without even thinking – for the second time that day – I followed through the gates and onto the vast driveway.

What had I just done? I couldn't turn around. What was I going to say? I had to do something and if I was nervous before it was nothing to how I felt now. I got out, grabbed my crutches and went over to the man. Straight away I didn't think I had the right person. He was younger than I had imagined and so once again I decided to blag it. "Hi," I said, "I'm Leanne." He smiled and seemed really pleasant and I think the fact I was one-legged on crutches made me appear innocent and non-threatening. "Sorry to bother you…is Tony around?" I continued, still trying to

sound as though I knew what I was talking about. "Sorry, no…he's at friends this evening. He'll be back later though. Have you got his mobile number?" Again, without thinking I replied: "Oh, sorry, I haven't got it on me," which wasn't really a lie – because I didn't have it on me. The fact I didn't have it at all was another matter! The man kindly gave me his father's number and with that I turned to leave.

My adrenaline was now truly pumping as I drove home but the excitement stopped me and I was ready, there and then, to take the chance that all day I'd been building up to. I pulled the car into a dark Sainsbury's car park and clutching the number in one hand and my phone in the other I dialled. My hands were shaking and after I realised there would be no answer I shut off the call. In a strange way I was quite relieved. I decided to send him a text.

I wanted something punchy, not a "sales-like" message which he would no doubt delete straight away, so I started by introducing myself and decided not to mention the words fundraising, charity or money. I said that I had a business proposition for him – one that would mean a lot

to us both and I just wanted to take him out to discuss it. I found being more forthright in a text much easier and was able to keep it cool. I made it sound as though if he'd be mad not to text me back. I put down my phone and drove home where I literally sprang through the door to tell Paul my news.

I really didn't know whether in fact he would actually get back to me and I wondered whether someone as successful as him would even bother with a small fry like me. Just as I was beginning to think how else I could find a sponsor my phone flashed. I had a message. My heart skipped a beat – was it him? Would he really have taken the time to text me back? Or, was it a "get lost" text? I didn't know if my heart could take it – either way. I flipped my phone open and my hand shook as I saw it was from him. Squinting through my anticipation I read the text aloud to Paul. It read: "Hello Leanne. Well, if you have a proposal for me I guess I'll have to take you out for breakfast on Friday." I couldn't believe it. I couldn't believe the words I was reading on the screen and read it over and over again just to make sure I wasn't dreaming. Paul and I were buzzing with excitement – I had just pulled off

another blag. We arranged to meet and I wanted to be three things. I wanted to be professional. I wanted to be serious, but I also wanted to be myself – which perhaps negated the other two! I knew he wouldn't just agree – perhaps he would be a hard nut to crack – and I didn't want him to think that I was some lunatic with a cheesy idea for raising some money. Over the following few days leading up to the meeting I prepared my pitch and did my research. I was determined to impress.

When Friday morning arrived I put on my best suit, highest black sleek heel as I didn't want the sympathy vote and I wanted to come across as a young, normal professional. I didn't plaster on the make-up as I wanted to come across as elegant and I dusted off my black briefcase as I stood outside the restaurant waiting his arrival. I got there early and hoped I was creating the right impression. I had no idea what this man looked like, but I knew he would obviously recognise me. That is one good thing about only having one leg – it's easy to describe yourself. I suddenly caught sight of a spectacular bright red Porsche driving through town. It had a personalised number plate – it was him. My heart felt as though it

would leap from my chest at any second. I wanted to race to the loo to calm my nerves but I knew this was my one and only chance and I wasn't about to blow it. But I was also partly relieved. You can never guarantee that someone is going to turn up and here he was – it was showtime.

You know how some people have a certain air about them? He did. He was charming and surprisingly young for someone so successful and the fact that I found him quite attractive helped as I felt at ease with him almost instantly. I shook his hand firmly. It was what I'd been taught to do and I was determined not to shake hands, trip on my crutches and fall flat on my face. That was a fear that worried me constantly when I was in certain situations but I didn't want it to become a reality then and there. We sat at a table and he ordered breakfast.

I am someone that has always had an appetite and I have to be in hospital severely ill or under an anaesthetic for me not to eat. I knew my friends would laugh when they heard that I ordered two pieces of brown toast and a glass of fruit juice. Despite the fact I could smell the yummy bacon and sausages, I ordered toast. I

was fairly nervous and I didn't want to end up with egg on my face – so to speak.

I began my briefing by telling him a little about myself and how I had lost my leg. I told him the circumstances that had led to my quest for money and he seemed interested and chatty as I went on to tell him about the spectacular ball I was planning at the biggest attraction in the South West. He seemed impressed that I had secured such a venue and as he seemed more and more intrigued, my confidence grew and grew. He asked me what I had planned already and I explained I was selling tickets and had set up a website. I'd already managed to secure a number of excellent prizes for raffles and I also wanted to hold a grand draw. As well as the great evening I had my heart set on I knew he would understand when I told him that I needed to raise some money. He continued to ask question after question and I could sense he was definitely interested. I went on to explain that I was looking for a sponsor for the event and then I described the benefit that I thought his companies might glean if he agreed to sponsor it.

He said he loved my idea and what I was doing. He wanted to think about it but said: "Aim high Leanne...if

you are going to make this much money, aim high." His words rang in my ears as we agreed to meet again in a couple of weeks and I said farewell to this man that I had learned to respect in a matter of minutes. I was pleased that I had seemingly managed to impress him.

Fresh from the meeting there was no stopping me. It was just the push I needed and I was determined to "knock him out" with even more amazing ideas the next time I saw him. As well as selling the tickets I decided to go up market and offer corporate tables to businesses for £1,000 per table. Now, to me, it seemed like a massive gamble. It was a lot of money to ask for, so I needed to impress still further – I wanted to blow people's socks off. I secured a special VIP area overlooking the biomes and worked with the catering staff at Eden to provide an exquisite menu for the special guests. Again, this meant a big personal outlay for me, and I felt under increasing pressure as my credit cards began mounting up. This would either turn into the most magical event ever or it would ruin me.

The VIP area boasted several exclusive tables for businesses where I knew companies would invite their

important clients. I was thinking perhaps lawyers, business partners and associates and clients that were willing to spend some money. I reasoned that if you could afford to buy a table for the evening for £1,000 then you could afford a few raffle tickets. For the VIP room I organised an amazing entertainer called Martyn Lucas who had recently performed on *Stars In Their Eyes* as Freddie Mercury. I had strict instructions on how the room should be laid out which was to be decorated tastefully and elegantly. There would be white linen on the tables and thousands of tiny white lights to adorn the huge windows which overlooked the biomes. Eden had already agreed to "light" the biomes and I knew it would look spectacular.

But the VIP area wasn't going to bring in a huge amount of money. Although the tables would be expensive for those who bought them, I still had a lot of money – totalling several thousands of pounds – to spend on a variety of things including meals, wine and entertainment. I decided that along with a raffle I would once again organise an auction. It had been so successful at the Alverton that I knew I had to ask Philip if he could help again. He kindly agreed and it was then down to me to

BELOW

Before and after –
above the knee
amputation
in London.

Photos above and opposite: Damon Taylor

RIGHT

Always supportive,
Gran and Gramps.

BELOW

Me with local
Businesses and
dressed in blue, Susie
Carter (a journalist who
has been with me on
this crazy journey).

ABOVE

Eden support – Even when I
was in hospital my family rallied
round to keep the campaign
rolling (above left, Rachael
Collier, friend, Auctioneer Philip
Buddell, Mum, Chris holding
Maisie who was only a few
weeks old, Dad and Paul.

Photo: CameraCraft

ABOVE

Body Shop Girls – I felt
like a Queen being
pampered by the
amazing supporters of
Girls Night In.

ABOVE LEFT

My brother with my
niece following her birth
in May 2005.

ABOVE RIGHT

Nathan and Richard –
One of our 'nights in'
with a takeaway and
a DVD.

LEFT

My darling niece, Maisie
and me.

LEFT

Me and Nathan.

BELOW LEFT

My first trip to London – I was nervous and excited all in one!

BELOW RIGHT

London here we come! One small step for Man, one giant leap for Leanne!

ABOVE

With the Jade's PA
finalists (from left:
Rebecca, me,
Chantelle, Emma, Tara,
Caroline and Eric).

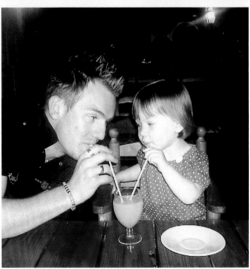

ABOVE

Best of friends, Charlie and I.

LEFT

The ties that bind – I'm so proud of my younger brother Chris who is an amazing Dad to our darling Maisie.

RIGHT

Me at Atlantic FM with presenter Alison Holland, doing some Radio interviews promoting the DVD.

**BELOW
LEFT TO RIGHT**

Getting a kiss from Russell Brand in Leicester Square – Me and Jade – Posing with Ricardo from Channel 4's *The Salon*.

ABOVE
Travelling the world and promoting the 'Leanne' brand, one leg, backpack and crutches.

MIDDLE
Smile!! Loving the camera.

LEFT
From Cornwall to LA (Leanne follows her dream and loves every second).

ABOVE LEFT TO RIGHT

Me and Alicia Duvall – Me and those Cheeky Girls (who can tell us apart?) – Me with Sting's ex-chef, Eric.

RIGHT

Some magazine clippings.

Wednesday October 18 2006 ● STAUSTELLVOICE ●
www.staustellvoice.co.uk

NEWS 3

VOICE EXCLUSIVE: BEHIND THE COURAGE OF ST STEPHEN GIRL BIDDING TO BE JADE'S PA

'It's been a rollercoaster ride, from lying in Mount Edgcumbe Hospice feeling like I wanted to die to attending a celebrity party in Leicester Square. I am trying to make the best of a bad situation, I'm really positive and aiming for the

SOMETHING IN COMMON Amputees Leanne and Heather Mills, former wife of Sir Paul McCartney

● WESTERN MORN

28 ● WESTCOUNTRY NEWS

Women of achievement ar

Within a few days Cornwall's first ever Women of Achievement winners will be unveiled. Petra Mann reports on the hopes of some of the contenders

● COMMUNITY ROLE: Maggie Parke

● INSPIRATIONAL: Leanne Grose

"The standard of the entries was incredible, which made our job very hard.

ABOVE
More magazine clippings.

phone around to see what companies could let me have for the auction.

To say I was blagging on the streets in my quest is an understatement. I spent an entire day in Plymouth starting at the top of the city and working my way through every single shop. I told them my story and asked if they would spare anything – anything at all – for the cause. Success was varied. My excitement went off the scale when I managed to secure a beautiful pair of amber earrings. I also managed to get vouchers and paintings. But there were some shops that refused. Even having been rejected I managed to smile as I thanked various staff for their time. It was particularly soul-destroying and it wasn't an easy task. I didn't expect anything, but I was forever hopeful and I wondered if they were asked a lot to donate things.

I think that a certain amount of my good luck and fortune asking people for things was because they could see that I'd got off my backside and was willing to try. I didn't send a standard letter, I went and met people face to face and I think that many people actually warmed to the personal touch. Yes, it was hard when I was turned

down and it certainly added to the rollercoaster of a ride I was experiencing. I sometimes felt as if I wanted to give up as I repeated the same story over and over again. Even hearing myself speak the words was driving me crazy, but I would gather my thoughts and remember what it was all about. I wanted to change my life and I wanted to make having a shower a possibility thereby making my life so much easier as well as enabling me to go to the toilet in private.

That night, exhausted from all the talking and effort I'd put into the day, I returned home and showed Paul and my family the mountain of goodies I had managed to collect. From a rug to jewellery from wine to beauty vouchers I sat back and felt proud of my achievements. I was so grateful to everyone that had been incredibly generous to me that day and spent the evening writing my "thank you" letters. I wanted them all to know how much easier my life would be and that their help was taking me one step closer to my goal.

The plans were certainly taking shape. I had managed to find a great live band called Tequila to play in the main biome. They were really popular and Clive, one of the

JUST A *Step*

band members, was the husband of my boss at work. The entire band agreed to play free of charge for the whole evening and I was over the moon. I had also arranged for a large steel band to play as guests entered the Eden Project and it was part of my dream come true. I have always loved steel bands so for one to be at the event was incredible. I also managed to find some fire-eaters who would walk around Eden on stilts to entertain the guests and I was even more amazed when I found a dance company with professional dancers who were prepared to come along. There was also going to be a spectacular chocolate fountain along with a balloon company who agreed to build an archway over the entrance so that people would walk under a large canopy of balloons.

I had so many other ideas and the whole thing was becoming more and more exciting. It was all beginning to fall into place and people were getting on board with the project and sharing in my excitement. The only thing I was running on was adrenaline. I was still working full time and determined not to let slip that the pain in my stump was still really bad. "Keep going!" I often told myself. "It will be worth it in the end. You've come this far – you can't give up."

Then everything flipped around again when at 1.00am the phone rang. I hate that feeling when the phone goes in the middle of the night. I was almost afraid to pick it up, but I answered: "Hello." I was nervous waiting for a voice to respond. It was my mum: "Kate's gone into labour and she's fine...Chris is with her." The feeling was amazing and I wanted to race to the hospital nearby to give them both a hug, but I waited.

Two hours later and the phone rang again. This time I grabbed it quickly to hear my brother tell me that I was an auntie and that they'd had a little girl. The feeling of euphoria I had was incredible. I cried as he told me excitedly that she was called Maisie Louise Grose (Louise is also my second name) and I couldn't wait to see them all. But I'd have to wait for a few hours yet. If it had been up to me I'd have thrown some clothes on and raced to the hospital to be with them but I knew they needed to be alone and visitors in the middle of the night were probably not allowed. The next morning couldn't happen quickly enough when I officially woke up as an auntie.

I had to go to Eden first for yet another meeting to

check that everything was running smoothly and as the hospital's 3.00pm visiting time arrived I knew I'd soon be meeting my niece for the first time. I called Chris to make sure everything was alright and he came to meet me in the car park to walk in with me. It was strange, although he was my younger brother, he no longer seemed that way. He was a man, and now of course, a dad. As we walked into the ward, the curtain was around Kate and the baby, and as I approached I tried to muffle the sound of the clacking crutches on the hard floor. We walked around the curtain and there was Maisie with whom I instantly fell head over heels in love. I tried hard to quash the tears of happiness and then they asked me if I wanted to hold her.

I love children, but as she wasn't mine I felt a bit nervous about holding such a tiny baby. I had Isaac in my life – the son of my best friend, Charlie, and he felt like a nephew, and there were also my younger cousins, but holding Maisie for the first time was one of the most amazing experiences I've ever had. I was nervous, but I was careful to hold her head properly and I simply looked at the beautiful, precious little girl. I knew I would love her always. Maisie's arrival was one of the most positive

things that had happened for a long while. Mum and dad settled into their role as grandparents with ease and Chris had developed from your average teenager into a natural father. He was excellent at nappy changing and having Maisie in his life seemed to help him grow into an adult. He was extremely hands on in every way.

I was still making several trips to the hospital to see pain specialists, oncologists, physiotherapists and doctors. They were all trying to find a way of helping the pain, but the only way I could really control the muscle pain and agony I was experiencing was to gulp the morphine provided. The trouble was that it left me desperately tired and I tried with all my might to make it through the day without morphine. I knew I was becoming more and more low in myself and the reserves that usually helped me inside were beginning to run dry. I knew though I was going to pull this off if it killed me. I prepared myself for my follow-up meeting with Tony. I left work having been wished luck by my colleagues and found that the nerves had kicked in again.

We met for breakfast again and I opted for the second time for the toast and fruit juice. We began the meeting

straight away and I explained all the things I had arranged and what I'd been doing for two weeks. I even told him about all the prizes and services that I'd managed to blag people into letting me have. The smile on his face told me he was impressed and he agreed to sponsor the event. I tried really hard not to look desperate but I was up there on cloud nine. I joked with him that he'd been "making me sweat" and he told me he wanted me to work for it – he needed to know I was serious and that simply made me feel even more proud of my achievements. Knowing that he believed in me and that I wasn't someone who wanted something for nothing and his recognition of that fact made me feel extremely pleased.

"Now, Leanne…about these auction lots," he began. He was impressed that another local businessman had kindly donated his villa in Spain for a holiday as well as giving me the use of his printing business to produce all the flyers and tickets. He was equally impressed with the executive box I'd managed to get for a Manchester United game at Old Trafford. I'd done it on my own. I'd hunted down an amazingly generous man who had agreed to the use of the executive box and I'd also been given a holiday

to New Zealand not to mention the beautiful pieces of artwork and other unique things. Not bad for a young, one-legged girl with some gumption and a desire for a shower. "I have some more lots to add to the list," he continued.

To my mind he had already done so much. He was going to sponsor the event and he'd given me the boost I needed by telling me to: "Reach for the stars." "Are you ready?" he asked as I grabbed my pen, unsure of what else could possibly be offered. "The first thing I'm offering is a brand new conservatory." I tried hard not to let my jaw hit the floor – I just couldn't believe that anyone could be this generous. "The use of my helicopter to fly four people to London for the day." By this time I had no feeling left in my good leg. Was I dreaming? "And, then of course, you need a star prize…a real finale to the auction. You need something that will really bring in the cash." I didn't know what else could top all this. I really didn't. "The use of my private Lear jet for eight people to be flown anywhere in the world for a holiday."

I had stopped writing on my pad. My hand no longer seemed to work and I could not believe my ears. I just

couldn't put the feelings I had into worlds. I was completely overwhelmed and I knew I didn't have the words to cover it. "It had better be a bloody good night," he said as we finalised the details and headed outside.

"Would you like a lift anywhere?" he asked kindly. Normally I'd have said no. I don't like to trouble anyone, but seeing the shiny red Porsche sitting there I couldn't resist. "Are you sure that would be okay?" I asked with a beaming smile on my face as he opened the door. On the journey back to my office I loved chatting to the man that I found fascinating and incredibly charming. His world amazed me and I was interested in how he had worked hard all his life. That car journey made me realise that I too was capable of anything if I wanted it badly enough – I could actually go out and get it.

As we pulled into the car park I was praying that everyone would be near the windows – not that I'm a complete poser or anything – it's just that it was a beast of a car and I felt like a million dollars travelling in it. He was the perfect gentleman and got out to open the door for me. It was so low that I really had to launch myself up so I joked with him not to look up my skirt. He giggled

and I was pleased that I could be myself with him. I kissed him on the cheek and said I would keep him up-to-date with progress. I would look forward to seeing him there and as he drove off I had a feeling about what I wanted from my future and it was the drive to succeed.

I spent absolutely ages telling my friends and family about what happened, but I was choosy in who I told as he'd asked me not to make a big thing of what he was prepared to help me with. It was just another reason to find him truly amazing. Now that there were so many incredible prizes I couldn't wait to make the evening spectacularly special. I spent time with Philip and his wife Linda producing a professional booklet as the prizes for the auction were "something else" and deserved to be presented in the best way possible.

But just as things were beginning to go exceptionally well, my health took another turn for the worse. I had been aware for some time that things had been building but I tried to ignore the fact that I was feeling more and more unwell. Things came to a head though when I had to be admitted to a pain rehabilitation centre at the Stanmore Hospital. I was sent kicking and screaming as I

still had an enormous amount to do for the ball and it was only three weeks away. I felt I couldn't afford to be gone and being the control freak I had turned out to be over the event I found it difficult to accept that enough was enough. I had desperately wanted to do every single thing myself, but the pain was so bad that every time I open my mouth to speak it was if I would be sick with the pain that was coursing through my body.

I went alone to London, leaving a list of contacts with strict instructions for my family and friends who pulled together to continue with the plans. I'm not usually prone to stress but I would say that this was one of the most stressful times in my life. I felt helpless being in hospital knowing that there was absolutely nothing I could do about it. I was admitted to a special ward in the rehab clinic and was due to face two weeks of intensive treatment which would consist of medication trials, physiotherapy on a daily basis, various exercises and even counselling. It was kind of like "Butlins for the sick" but without the fun part.

Each day had a schedule and mornings began early and appointment followed appointment. I knew deep

down it was something I had to accept and go through and that I couldn't bury my head in the sand any more. I began to think that the quicker I got on with it the quicker I would get home. I was again blessed with the patients with whom I shared a ward. They were a great bunch of people and the department was separated into two units: one for men and one for women.

I met Sarah who was a few years younger than me who had problems with her shoulder from which I gathered she had suffered for an extremely long time, and then there was Bernie. Bernie was older and a real character. I felt instantly at ease around her and I discovered that she was suffering from MS and despite the brave face she put on things the illness was severely affecting her day-to-day life. Although never far from my mind, the ball had taken a back seat as I concentrated on getting better and attending all the sessions and appointments that were booked for me. I enjoyed Sarah's and Bernie's company and we also made friends with several guys on the other unit. It really was a hospital stay like no other but I felt at home with the people around who, like me, were suffering with great pain but managing to smile through it somehow.

Every morning I would be picked up by Ray, a member of staff, who would take me to physiotherapy for a gruelling workout. I went to each appointment in a wheelchair and as he pushed me along I began to learn some things about him. He was originally from Ghana and had the biggest smile I think I've ever seen. You could hear Ray laughing as he made his way down the corridor before you ever saw him. He would collect me and he, along with the treatments and my new found friends, certainly made the stay more bearable. But, there were times when I hated it. When it was time for an injection or a scan or the physiotherapist wanted me to stretch that little bit too far and I would end up writhing in agony. Then there was one day that changed my perception on things.

We were taken in a convoy of wheelchairs to a gigantic specialist sports hall that boasted the most incredible facilities for those less able. One afternoon we had a scheduled swim and I couldn't wait. Looking in from outside it must have been a strange sight. There were around eight of us all with differing problems who were being helped into the swimming pool. I joked that we should be called the raggy dolls as we all had different

things wrong with us and I was humble around those who were with me as we all battled with our pain. As the water from the pool lapped over me I felt calm. Thoughts of the ball and the fundraising were much further from my mind and I began to let my body relax. The pool was fun and the help that the staff gave us to enjoy our time in there was exceptional.

After swimming we were asked if we wanted to do something more active. I was ready for anything at this point and certainly wanted to push myself to see what my body could actually do. When tennis was suggested I was on the verge of laughing. How on earth could I play tennis with one leg? Yes, it was something I had enjoyed before my amputation and I'd loved the thrill of bounding around a court, smashing the ball towards my opponent, but I had accepted that tennis would no longer be possible. Now someone was telling me it was.

We were wheeled to the courts and each given a racket. We were going to play doubles and we partnered according to our problems. I was partnered with a lovely guy called Terry who had the full use of his legs but had problems with his arm. We were playing against Bernie

and her partner and as the whistle sounded for the start of the game I had a strange feeling that just washed over me. One I had not felt for an incredibly long time. I was being competitive and the adrenaline rush simply made me ecstatic.

As we started to play the tears began gently rolling down my face and I felt normal for the first time in a long time. I had been given a taste of what my life had been like, so quickly wiping away the tears I got stuck into the game. Okay, so we weren't playing at Wimbledon or to that kind of standard, but it just didn't matter. I had played tennis. I couldn't wait to phone everyone back home to tell them of my achievement. On the way back to the ward the physiotherapist pushed me along a different corridor and through another gym. "Excuse me," I said as I turned my head around to face her. "Who's in there?" I asked as I pointed through another door and into the gym. There were several men – all young – leaning against a board. Their feet were slightly off the floor and their heads were resting on the edge of this wooden vertical platform. A fan was blowing into their faces and everyone seemed to be smiling. I know I was just being nosey but it was something

I hadn't seen before and I was curious. "They've all broken their backs," came the reply. "They can't walk and they enjoy having some time in that position because it's a change from lying in bed or being in a wheelchair," she continued.

As I looked at all the young men I felt a pang in my heart. I was crying on the inside as the physiotherapist returned me to the ward and I realised how truly lucky I really was. That afternoon marked a turning point for me seeing those young bodies with broken backs and I knew then that I had to remain positive and focused and thankful for all that I actually had. Like clockwork, there was Ray arriving to collect me. I looked forward to seeing him each morning and I liked listening to his stories as he wheeled me to yet another appointment. He was going to university to study to become a pharmacist and I had real admiration for him.

On my final day at the rehab clinic I was poked and prodded and thoroughly analysed before being told I was ready to go home. I had gained so much from my stay at Stanmore and it had opened my eyes. It was as if I had had an enriching experience while being there and I

hugged everyone on the ward and wished Ray all the very best with his studies along with saying my goodbyes to the doctors and nurses who had looked after me. On the long journey back I changed from relaxed mode to ball mode. I had been in contact with all those who were helping me as I was anxious to know that everything was running smoothly in my absence. I knew they were doing a sterling job and I was surprised when I saw a piece in the local paper which had drummed up interest and support for the event. There was a good picture of my parents and Paul along with Chris, Kate and my niece Maisie as well as Philip and Rachael.

There was just enough time for me to find a stunning new dress and finalise all the details. The girls who had so eloquently walked down the catwalk at the previous event had agreed to be helpers for the ball and I had bought strawberries, Cornish clotted cream and handmade chocolates for them to walk around with and offer to the guests. As the day arrived, my adrenaline began to pump and I was ready and raring to go. That morning I boldly told myself that it was either going to be the greatest night on earth or the biggest disaster! Time seemed to race by

as we spent the day setting everything up. I made list after list of jobs to be done which eventually came in handy while I spent the day with my phone glued to my ear. My organisational skills were certainly being tested to the limit. The calm I had experienced at the hospital had all but vanished as I raced around putting the finishing touches to the evening. There was even a lavish red carpet for the guests to walk over at the entrance – I wanted it to be magical.

I raced home to get changed. Isn't it typical that the one time you want to look simply stunning you don't have enough time? I entered the house, sweating streams and jumped in the bath. I was very tired as I was on so many different drugs that I was feeling incredibly sleepy. It was a catch 22 situation. I needed the drugs to keep the pain at bay, but the more I had to take the more exhausted I became. I needed to battle on however ready for one of the biggest nights of my life. As I arrived back at Eden a number of people were racing around putting the last minute touches to the lavish event. As guests walked down the red carpet they would be greeted with a glass of champagne and the VIP guests would be ushered into the

corporate room while other guests would be escorted to the land train where they would travel in style on a sunny summer's evening to the biomes.

I decided not to eat that evening. I wanted to greet every single guest myself, after all, they were paying to help me out! I wanted to stand tall as I shook hands with everyone but eventually the ridiculously high-heeled silver stiletto I was wearing on my right foot got the better of me and I ended up sitting on a high chair. I must admit though, that I felt a bit like a princess in my extravagant pale blue dress which flowed in the slight breeze.

As people arrived I was pleasantly surprised by how much effort the guests had gone to. Ladies were dressed in ball gowns with their hair and make-up beautifully done while the men looked dashing in their tuxedos. Whereas I had been doubtful, wondering if a black tie event would put people off, I now had absolutely no regrets. I thought everyone looked stunning. I hugged, kissed and thanked more than 600 people who passed by me on their way to what I hoped would be an exceptional evening. There were friends, family and strangers all walking past me and

speaking to me. I felt incredibly special – like a celebrity – especially when the Chief Executive of Carrick arrived.

As the last guests filtered through I was asked by journalists from local newspapers to go to the balcony for press photographs. I know I only had one leg and I couldn't walk, but I really felt as if I glided that night. I thought that the girls' night in had been spectacular, but as I stood on the balcony at the Eden Project on a balmy summer's night, overlooking the lit biomes while listening to Hammered Steel, the steel band and hearing the laughter of guests as they mingled and chatted I found myself covered in goose bumps. Never in my wildest dreams had I imagined it would all be this perfect.

I spent my time moving between guests and when I entered the VIP room filled with corporates I glanced over at Tony, my millionaire, who seemed to be thoroughly enjoying the evening. I felt immensely proud introducing him to my family and he was as gracious as ever. Actually I thought he looked extremely sexy in his black tie. As pudding was served he and my dad stepped outside. I had no idea what was going on but when he returned, dad just said they'd had a chat. I didn't have time to query him as

I found myself busy talking to staff at Eden about various things to ensure that the evening kept running smoothly.

Once the meal was finished I invited the VIP guests to board the land train so that they could come down to the spectacular biomes to join the main event. I sat opposite Tony on the train and just watched him as he surveyed everything around him. I think he was impressed with what I'd achieved and I wanted him to be proud of me. I'd only known him for a short time, but his admiration that I'd managed to pull off this event was incredibly important to me. As the VIP guests entered the biomes I found that the evening was taking its toll on me. What with the pain and the tiredness I was suddenly finding it difficult to move about and was relieved when a security guard with a wheelchair was waiting for me. I wouldn't ordinarily have wanted to admit I needed one, it would be like admitting defeat, but I had to accept it and I gratefully got into the chair. As we entered the throng of people, sipping wine and enjoying the entertainment, they began to clap as I was pushed through them. I didn't want to ruin my make-up so I tried very hard not to cry – the whole thing was overwhelming. Wine was flowing, the chocolate

fountain was a huge success and then the professional dancers began their routine.

Dancing was followed by the auction and to be honest I was slightly nervous by this time. I was worried – as I had been before – that this part would be dry and boring. How wrong was I? Philip stood tall in the middle of the massive crowd and basically worked his socks off. He was magical and I realised that I wasn't paying attention to what the lots were selling for as I was more interested in whether they sold at all. The room was suddenly tense with excitement and people were trying to hear the lots. The auction booklets were an excellent idea and then, through the crowd, I spotted Charlie who just winked at me.

My ears suddenly pricked up when one of the pieces of art I thought would sell for £20 or £30 went for hundreds and the trip to New Zealand for thousands. The atmosphere by this time was electric. The final lot, for the flights on the Lear jet, donated by my millionaire proved to be intense as there were around six parties or so who were bidding at up to £7,000. I felt as though my heart was going to escape and jump out of my chest I was so nervous. It was a surreal experience as Philip worked his magic on the bidders – as

they say: "You had to be there!" As Philip brought down the hammer and shouted: "Sold!" the Lear jet lot went for more than £8,000.

From the wheelchair I managed to catch a quick glimpse of the mystery guest who had eventually won the lot. He discreetly stepped back and rejoined his table and no one else saw who it was. If I had had two legs, I'm not sure I'd have been able to feel them anyway at this point. I was so overwhelmed, but I had to get a grip fairly quickly as I announced for everyone to gather outside for a surprise.

Okay, so some would call me extravagant, but as I always claimed, I wanted the evening to remain a long lasting memory for those who were there. As the guests huddled outside I gave "the sign" and the beautiful firework display began showing off the biomes in all their glory. The dark night made it special for the whooping crowd and as I sat near the front of them in the wheelchair my eyes glazed over. As I looked up into the sky I had so many thoughts whirring around my head. What had happened? I thought about the loss of my leg and wondered if I'd ever be able to walk again. Would I get

better? Would I see my gorgeous new niece grow up? Quietly I whispered: "Granny, I love you…I hope you are here."

Mum must have known what I was thinking as she approached me with dad. They both hugged me and we watched in silence as the fireworks continued. After the display people filtered back into the biomes and Tequila belted out their first song. The whole evening had been filled with entertainment and it was an emotional night for me. Everyone seemed to be having a wonderful time as they danced their arses off!

Believe it or not I was now relieved. I'd made my speech to the large crowd of people and had managed to thank everyone I needed to. I wanted each and every one of them to know that they had all contributed to something amazing that night – they had changed my life. I also had a few surprises myself, one of which was a letter that Philip kindly read to everyone. It was from Canda Hedges, my mum's boss who was on holiday and unable to attend. She had written that I was a fighter and that although she wanted everyone to enjoy themselves she hoped they would give a little to make my dream come

true. Her praise in the letter humbled me and she wrote that as she couldn't be there in person she was donating £1,000 to my fundraising account. It came as a huge surprise to me.

As the dancing continued I was overwhelmed with people coming up and hugging, kissing and congratulating me on what had been an incredible evening. Linda, Philip's wife, had quietly been totting up the amount from the auction and came over to announce that: "We'd done it!" There was enough for my life-changing downstairs shower room! The girls from work and I just hugged and hugged and I couldn't believe the achievement. I felt well and truly loved that night and there was only one person missing, but I knew she was looking down on me and smiling.

I was pulled in so many different directions as people wanted to say goodbye and have a chat before leaving. There were even a few businessmen in tears, holding me and telling me it was the best evening they had ever been to. The kindness of everyone was fantastic and Specsavers in St Austell had even donated two Tag Heuer watches that were prizes in a special raffle. As people began to filter out

and I had kissed as many people as I could I knew I had one last thank you to make.

"It was you…wasn't it?" I said to Tony. I looked into his eyes and I could see that he felt emotional. "I saw you bid for your own jet," I said. "But, you've already given me so much…" "You've done it!" he replied as he held my face in his hands "And, the jet…that's for you, that's for you and your family." I held his face too and kissed him. He had known all along how much I needed to raise and I later discovered that the "quiet word" he'd had with dad was to ensure that all the money I needed to raise would be raised that night. I turned to Paul, my parents and Chris and everyone had tears in their eyes. There were no words to describe how I felt.

"I would have always helped you out, Leanne," he said smiling, "but I wanted you to work for it." "I wouldn't want it any other way," I replied as I hugged him once again.

To say the night had been a success was an understatement. I felt proud and privileged to be in a room with so many amazing people who were there for me. The following days went by in a haze and I thought I must have dreamed the whole thing as I played the scenes of that

night over and over again in my head. Although I was tired, what I'd achieved with the help of so many people is something that will live with me until the day I die.

The organising, panicking and worry were finally over and I was so excited when Paul called the builder to start work on the new extension. Kevin Tregunna was the builder who got the job and he was great. He fully understood my needs and pushed the project forward to ensure that I would have the shower room I longed for as soon as possible. Every day there would be more bricks going together, more cement being mixed and more materials being delivered. I kept everyone at the office up to date with progress. They had all helped so much to make this happen and I felt very blessed. But sometimes working with friends had its down sides.

They really knew me and no matter how hard I tried at times to hide the pain I was in or how bad I was actually feeling they realised. Jacquie and Charlie would comment if I was taking morphine and I knew they worried about me. By now, the pain was so bad that I was also taking Kettamine in addition to the usual drugs as I was finding it increasingly difficult to get through the day. I always

turned up for work but some days my eyes would be glazed over and my body felt numb. I felt so bad that I reckoned that if someone stuck a knife in me I wouldn't even feel it. After a long time of Charlie, Jacquie, Shena, Sandra, Rachael and Melissa badgering me about getting some help, I finally decided to call Macmillan.

As always someone was with me quickly and came to my home to assess how I was doing. I thought they'd have a chat, have another look at my medication etc, but this time it was more serious. "I think it would be best if we put you in a hospice for a while, Leanne," came the assessment. "That way, they can look after you properly on a full time basis."

My heart sank. Was I that bad that I needed to go into a hospice? Was I going to die? Had they not told me something? I was panicked by an overwhelming fear. I had no choice and I had to accept that I was getting worse and on top of everything else I was exhausted. I had already felt guilty about all the things that Paul needed to do at home and I knew it worried my parents and my friends. I had to give in. Mum and dad took me to the hospice on a Saturday morning but I told them I didn't want them to

come in with me. It was, once again, something I wanted to do alone. I didn't want to put them or anyone else through any more experiences and I didn't want them to see me in a hospice. I thought it was a place where people went to die – but I was completely mistaken.

As I went inside with my bags I was greeted by a beautiful stream of fish, there were lots of smiles from staff and bright pictures hung on the walls. It certainly wasn't what I had been expecting and all thoughts of grey depressing corridors were now wiped from my mind. I was shown to my room by a lovely caring nurse who took my bags and placed her arm around my shoulder. My room was also unexpected. I had a television in the corner, a balcony overlooking magnificent gardens and an ensuite bathroom – in fact it was better than many hotels I'd stayed at.

As I unpacked the nurse went through what would be happening while I stayed at Mount Edgecombe. They would focus on my pain and try and get it under control. I was due to stay for one week and although that seemed like a long time I had done it before and I knew I could cope and do it again. The nurse left me to finish

unpacking and I took the time to gather my thoughts. I decided that I was going to make the best of not such a great situation and would definitely put a smile on things. That evening, Paul, my parents and Chris all came to visit and I thought it would be the usual routine of smiling, acting fine and trying to mask the fear I still felt inside. But, as it turned out I met them at the door and was proud to show them around. It was beautiful, I was safe and being looked after and, that, after all, was what they wanted for me. Dad sat in the comfy reclining chair and we all snuggled up and watched television in my new room. "I can cope with this!" I told myself as I kissed them goodnight and said I'd see them the following evening.

The next day I was woken by another nurse who asked what I wanted for breakfast. I soon learnt that it wasn't like being in hospital and nothing about it was morbid. Granted, I was in a room on my own and didn't see other patients, some of whom were there because they were desperately ill and would live out their last days in the hospice, but that wasn't for me. I was there to live. I was there to get better and I was going to get back on track and go home.

The nurses weren't like hospital nurses either – they were more like friends. They would come into the room often and as I was the youngest patient by quite a bit they would come in for a girly chat and one day, when I was particularly unwell and weak, a lady came and did my hair. She washed it over the bath and spent time making it look pretty before my visitors arrived. It was a far cry from the night at Eden when I felt glamorous and special – Leanne – the Leanne I always wanted to be, but I had to accept that I wasn't always like that and finally, the mask was well and truly down as people were allowed to see the real Leanne who was poorly.

Days in the hospice were filled with massage – which I can highly recommend. It was fantastic and when the lady first massaged me I began to cry. It was pure emotion which seemed to come from somewhere I didn't recognise deep within myself. I think I felt complete happiness that for once my body was being treated so gently and it was like having a break. I had put my body through the mill and I had pushed myself to lead a normal life – I had purposefully led people to think I was absolutely okay when deep down I knew that actually I wasn't. Just like in

hospital there were many people who came to visit me in the hospice but, to be honest, I was quite defensive. I had let down my guard and I had admitted defeat – for a while – and I didn't want everyone to see me like that. I was, at that time, in a world I had been trying to avoid for the past few years. I was looked after amazingly well and found I got on with all the staff, but there was nothing glamorous about it all. In fact, I was beginning to feel slightly institutionalised. Days were productive but as the doctors changed my drugs and did trials with different pills to try and tackle the pain I felt a big change in myself.

My words became slurred and I began to feel more and more "spaced out". Visitors would come and go and I didn't have the time or energy to be defensive anymore as I struggled to remember what I was saying. I was frightened. I had pain down my neck which was increasingly uncomfortable and I was incredibly anxious.

One evening I had a big group of visitors of my girlfriends from school. As I lay in my bed, looking awful, they entered all dressed up and obviously ready for a night out. It was lovely to see them and we chatted for a while about what they had all been up to. I hadn't seen any of

them for a while and it was great to catch up, but they told me they couldn't stop for long as they were meeting a group of other people at a local pub.

As I sat listening to Donna, Kay, Kelly, Lisa, Vicky and Laura I felt desperately sad. It wasn't their fault, it was probably me, but I felt separated from them by a million miles. We had all grown up together and laughed in the school playground, but as they were keen to get going for their night out and getting drunk, I was stuck in the hospice trying to get my life together. I was feeling ill and I was feeling tired. Deep down the visit upset me and when they left to go it was a real slap in the face that I couldn't go with them. It reminded me of how different things now were and all the things I couldn't do. But, it was entirely different with Charlie and Emma from work. Charlie as I've said had become like a sister to me and I felt that they both had more understanding for what I was going through. I also felt that they cared. They brightened my afternoons with their visits while they sat gossiping and munching on homemade cakes.

One afternoon I didn't feel as cheery as I waited for their arrival, and instead of sitting up in anticipation I was

lying down on the bed. The doctor was injecting drugs into a vein in my arm and I could barely see them through my drug-fuelled haze. I was slurring my words and they could instantly tell I'd taken a turn for the worse. The worry I could see in their expressions made me panic all the more. Did they know something I didn't? By the evening I was worse and the pain in my neck was unbearable. I was as high as a kite by the time my parents arrived and I was a slobbering wreck who was tense with fear. I didn't know how to control myself and I felt slightly psychotic. Mum tried to calm me and I pushed her away with some force.

I don't know why it happened and looking back I feel sick that I did it, but I truly didn't know what I was doing. Both my parents grabbed me and got me back into bed as the nurse entered and announced that Jacquie had come to see me. "I can't see her!" I shouted. "Okay…okay darling," mum said stroking my head. She went out to see Jacquie who was waiting in the foyer. She was gone for ages and I just felt sick. I counted Jacquie as a friend, but she was also my boss. What on earth must she be thinking? I was paranoid – but I felt as if everything was slipping away.

JUST A *Step*

I thought I was slipping away.

Mum had explained I was too ill to see anyone and Jacquie understood. The nurses suggested that mum stay with me that night and they set up a camp bed so she could remain with me. I kissed my dad goodbye and just as he was talking to mum, Paul and Chris arrived. But, by now I was floating above them all. I was looking down at my family and my head just didn't feel right. I knew my body was giving up and at that moment I was no longer frightened. I felt restful and I couldn't take any more pain. I wanted to sleep and I wanted to give in, but a small voice somewhere inside me was telling me not to give up. I looked down on my family again and I knew I couldn't give up fighting. I had to fight for them.

The whole night seemed to last forever and I was sick as I've never been sick before. I was constantly having to race to the loo where liquid poured out of almost every conceivable orifice. Mum just held me. She stroked my head and kissed me gently. Just knowing she was there was my saving grace. It helped me make it through the night although the following morning I still felt all wrong. Wrong is the only way to describe it. I didn't feel like

anything or anyone I recognised – I felt low and my body was weak and fragile.

Mum left early to go home and change because I sent her off. She was looking drained with worry. The pain in my neck just got worse and worse and the nurses were in and out constantly to check on me. Things had taken a massive turn and from feeling as if I was in a hotel-like room, the hospice had turned into a hospital. Another amount of drugs sent me to sleep for an hour or so but I woke up to see a look of shock on the face of one of the nurses. Everything happened really quickly after that. She left the room and was replaced by another nurse who held my hand: "We're calling your family," she said calmly. She was trying to keep me calm and reassure me. All I could think was: "What's gone wrong?" "We think you may have had a stroke in your sleep," she continued with concern. Instantly, I knew it was back. It had been 10 years since my first attack of Bell's palsy, and now, here it was again. I couldn't believe that life could treat me so cruelly.

My parents arrived swiftly and they knew, like me, exactly what it was. There was the droopy lip, the staring eye. They took me from St Austell to the hospital in Truro

and we collected Paul on the way. Now, I hadn't known Paul when I had last had Bell's palsy so I didn't know how he would react when he saw me. Dad pulled up outside the house and Paul came to the door. He took one look at me through the car window and said he had forgotten something inside. He raced back in and so mum and I followed. Paul was crying. "I'm fine Paul," I whispered in his ear. "I promise you that I will get over this." At that moment I didn't know whether I believed it myself or not but I knew it was what he needed to hear.

He held me close and I knew he was just as scared as I was. It was unsettling in a way as Paul had often not shown his emotional feelings around me. We all piled back in the car and drove to the hospital where they confirmed what we already knew – I had Bell's palsy. It was a devastating blow which took away part of my persona – I couldn't smile and that just wasn't me. The one week I was due to spend at Mount Edgecombe turned into nearly a month and over that time I became quite dependent. I felt as though I was swiftly losing my own identity and the days were long.

The staff were fabulous and I had regular visitors from

family, friends and the girls at work, but I missed my home, I missed my own bed and I missed my freedom. It was a struggle to get better and there were several trial runs at getting back to normality with Paul taking me home for the day. But within hours I would start shaking and break out in cold sweats which made me desperately panicky. He would have to drive me back to the hospice where I would be given something to calm me down. Then I felt safe again.

I thought I was losing my marbles and I knew that the amount of drugs I was taking were not just affecting the pain in my stump but my mind as well – I couldn't feel either. I decided that I would rather suffer more pain than feel like I did – I was slowly losing myself. As Charlie, Emma and little Isaac came to visit in the afternoon I told them I was scared.

"Right," said Charlie, "We're taking you home." At that moment something kicked in and "Yes!" I thought, I was ready to make a run for it. We spoke to nurses and they agreed so long as I felt up to it they were happy for me to have another trial. The three of us packed my bags and as you can imagine after a month's stay there was

quite a lot of stuff to pack along with goodies like chocolates and gifts. Rachael at work had even made me a "happy" and a "sad" face on either side of a stick that I could use to show how I was feeling when my mouth wasn't working. With the car loaded I was ready to go and I hugged everyone who had looked after me telling them all that I could do it this time. Then I was free.

It was a slow process once I got home but every day I was aware that I was getting better little by little. I tried hard to be positive and I went and had acupuncture for my face to help get it back to normal and I also went back to work to try and put some semblance of normality on things and to give me a routine. One thing that really helped to pick me up was that the extension was nearly finished and it was comforting having the builders around. They were part of the furniture by now and we joked as they worked. Each one was aware of how important the project was to me and they were pulling out all the stops in order to finish the building by Christmas.

Maisie was growing up and I loved having her around. She was so precious to me and I found that being with her made me forget all the other things that were going on in

my life. Paul was also close to Maisie and I also loved watching them play together. Things picked up and I forced myself to do things in order to get better – but it was tough. There would be setbacks and the biggest one was receiving a letter from London. It was from Evelyn's son Michael.

After Amy died I had desperately tried to get hold of Evelyn as I needed to know she was alright. I'd met Michael when his mother was in hospital but I thought it was strange to hear from him, not Evelyn. My eyes quickly scanned the page and my heart sank when I read what he had to say. Evelyn had died. Michael had discovered my address in his mother's personal things and he wrote to thank me for making her time at Stanmore more bearable. He thanked me for being her friend. I wrote back immediately and explained how blessed I felt to have met his mother. My thoughts were with them all. In a strange way, the deaths of both Amy and Evelyn gave me even more reason to fight. On one hand I was consumed with guilt – why was I still here when they were not? Maybe I should have gone too. But on the other it made me stronger and I told myself that I was here for a reason and that I had to

pick myself up and get on with the life that I had.

By Christmas, as promised, my extension was complete and the acupuncture was working. I was able to smile and I found I was happy. The same night that the building was finished and the fittings were installed I prepared myself for my first shower in nearly four years. I told Paul that I wanted to manage by myself and he discreetly allowed me to be on my own. I entered the shower and sat on the chair while the fresh water fell on my head and tricked down my body. It was an amazing feeling and I sat in the shower and cried. I had a mixture of both happy and sad feelings. I was happy to have once again managed to turn a corner and I was happy with all that I had achieved. I had worked hard but I was equally sad that I was reminded sitting on the special chair in my shower room that there were many things I was no longer able to do.

The next day I woke early with a mission on my mind. I wanted to ring the social worker who said I would never raise the money. I was quite excited. I wasn't going to be nasty and say: "I told you so!" The fact that I had raised the money had been front page news in *The West Briton*

and I knew that she already knew. But, I had to return something anyway. I drove the car with the unsightly commode on board and turned into the car park. I dialled the number and asked for some assistance. Obviously I couldn't carry it in myself so I wanted someone to help me.

"May I ask who's calling?" the lady on the other end said as she was about to put me through. I told her who I was and that I had come with the commode to hand it back. She knew who I was and I was put on hold. "Leanne...unfortunately she is unable to see you and has asked that you leave the commode in reception." "But, I can't carry it...I'm on crutches," I replied.

"Well, leave it outside in the car park and it will be collected," came the reply and with that she put the phone down. I was gobsmacked. They didn't even have the decency to come and collect it. I don't know what I was expecting but it was a damn sight more than that. I dumped the bloody commode in the car park and drove away feeling angry.

Chapter 8

Back to reality

With my new facilities I felt that I was clawing back a little of my old life. I had accepted that my leg had gone, there was no point in thinking about it all the time. I had to make the most of it and get on with my life. I was determined that that was what I would do. With Christmas gone – which was a fabulous time with my family where we'd all got up at 3.00am to open presents – and after a few days of feasting on turkey and Quality Streets I hit the January sales. After spending far too much time looking at myself in the mirrors in changing rooms I realised that I had, over the past few years, put on quite a bit of weight.

After four years sitting in a wheelchair or lying in bed recuperating after operations, while scoffing chocolates and not being able to walk, my body shape had changed and I hardly resembled the slim, fit netball player that I had once been. As with everything else that happened I didn't like I decided to change things and went along with

Charlie to a Slimming World class. It was the first time in 10 years that I had weighed and I wasn't happy when I looked down at the scales. I had had part of my body removed and I was still heavier than I wanted to be – what more did I have to do?

I knew that diet alone wasn't going to get me back to the weight I wanted to be so I looked at ways I could exercise. I went after work one day and bought the tracksuit, water bottle and trainers (well, one) and prepared myself to become a fitness guru. I went to a gym and felt quite nervous – I hadn't done anything like it for a long time. As I entered the fitness suite a deathly hush fell across the room as everyone's gaze was on me. But I ignored them and was determined with a fighting spirit that I could do it. I worked my way around the machines to find out what I could and couldn't do. The treadmill was a no no, and likewise the bike for obvious reasons. I was trying my best and the people around me were beginning to take interest. Soon I was having conversations with people and I began to gain in confidence.

I knew then I had made the right move and as soon as

I found something I could do I became excited. The rowing machine was my favourite and the feeling of working out was quite amazing. I was young and alive again. I also took up swimming which was something I'd always loved. Charlie and I would often go on a Monday and enjoy an evening in the pool and the jacuzzi. Fresh from the excitement I decided to go one stage further and began attending a yoga class. As well as getting fit again I was proving something to myself and, just as with Eden and all the operations, it gave me an inner strength which I intended to use to the full.

As I walked into my first class, all eyes were on me and the teacher looked quite apprehensive. I tried to put her at her ease by telling her that anything I couldn't do I'd make the best of and that I was willing to try anything. The class began and I knew that people were looking to see how I was coping. "Bend and stretch those knees," the teacher instructed and then to me she said: "Leanne, bend that knee...bend it!" I replied: "I can't bend that knee, I haven't got one!" My jovial comment fell like a lead balloon and the usual comic routine wasn't about to get me through this time. After class the teacher called me to

one side. "Thanks…I really enjoyed that," I said. She just held up her hands. "Sorry, Leanne, but I am simply not prepared to have an amputee in my class." I just didn't have the strength to argue and she obviously didn't want to give me a chance.

I thanked her and left with her words still ringing in my ears. I decided to try something else instead. Charlie was keen on aerobics and I thought I'd go along unsure of what to expect. I imagined a class full of people running around in lycra and headbands followed by skipping on the spot. To my immense relief it was nothing like that. As soon as I arrived the trainers, Amanda Torris and Angie Smith came over and hugged me. They were my kind of people and I jokingly asked them if they were up for a challenge. They most certainly were and I had a go at all the exercises and for the things I couldn't do I found an alternative way around it. The support I got from the rest of the class was fabulous and I went home feeling on cloud nine. I continued with the class which left me with an adrenaline high – my life was going well.

Maisie was learning more and more new things and mum and dad had finally gone on holiday. Paul and I were

meanwhile busy with work. I found I had a new addiction – exercise and so I thought I'd go out and buy a fitness DVD so that I could also exercise at home. I went to Woolworth's and looked at the 15 or so celebrity fitness DVDs on offer. I opted for the number one bestseller and couldn't wait to get home to try it out. I turned it on and sat down ready for the warm up.

Star jumps – okay, well that would be difficult but I thought I'd adapt my own kind. The next exercise was jumping up and down. Umm, also not that useful for me. As I scanned through the DVD I felt rising disappointment that so many exercises included were simply not possible for me to do. I had just wasted £20. Later that night as I made my way to bed I had another thought. Why not make my own fitness DVD? Perhaps it sounded a little off the wall – but why not? I wondered whether it was possible and if I had this problem I was sure that other people did too. I thought perhaps that others in the same boat as me would appreciate a DVD to help them regain fitness. My head – once again – was buzzing with my idea and I began to get rather excited about my new project.

I put together a plan, produced a website, made up

business cards and was determined to make it a success. Nothing was going to stop me and I wanted to reach for the stars. I wanted to achieve anything and everything I put my mind to. Just as I had done before by engineering my chance meeting with my millionaire, I didn't see why I couldn't do something similar with one of the biggest names in the country. I didn't want to sell a few DVDs in a local shop – I wanted this to be a new phenomenon which would help and encourage millions of people and for this to be something that could go some way to ridding the UK of a big taboo – amputees and disabilities in general.

The obvious choice was Max Clifford. He was someone I admired and he was powerful, successful and definitely somebody I thought should be on my side. Okay, reading this it may sound like it was a long shot but if I had one thing going for me it was determination. I did my research and found out where his offices were and noted down his contact details. I dialled the number and was nervous as I quickly ran over in my head what I was about to say.

"Good afternoon, my name is Leanne Grose and I'd like to be put through to Mr Clifford, please," I said confidently. "I'm afraid he's unavailable," came the reply

which didn't surprise me at all. "I don't know if you can help me?" I continued, and then changed my tack from professional to personal as I explained why I was phoning. The lady I spoke to was really helpful and seemed genuinely excited about my projects. I asked her for her details so I could email her and she promised she would pass on all my information to Max Clifford to see if he would consider meeting with me. I was getting there. I was extremely excited and couldn't wait to see how far I could take this. I had drawn up a professional proposal and written a flashy CV describing myself and my story. Within a couple of hours I received an email from Max's assistant telling me they were both really interested and I was asked if I could attend a meeting in Bond Street – could I! I was overjoyed and speechless. I had a couple of weeks to prepare. The girls at work were all excited for me and, having been successful with Eden, I was driven to do even bigger and better things.

During the day I was busy with my 9 to 5 job, while the evenings were taken up with my future. I was planning how to make it big but I still had a nagging feeling about my health. I knew, though, that there was no point in burying

my head in the sand and the thought of another scan, more treatment or another operation was scaring the hell out of me. I had an amazing oncologist called Dr Thompson who was kind and understanding. I felt that we connected which helped and there was also the specialist, Rachael, who was on my wavelength. She was exceptional in her care to help me manage the pain. After meeting with them both I returned to Stanmore for yet another scan and I was anxious for the entire trip. I had so much to look forward to that the thought of going down the "poorly" route once again was almost more than I could bear. I still had a massive fear of MRI scans but the staff at Stanmore were completely understanding and helped me get through. With the scan complete I had to see another specialist for the results and then, yet again, my heart sank. The tumour was back.

I had fibromatosis forming at the end of my stump which grew like ivy around the bones damaging them and damaging me. I didn't know why it was continuing to happen. After several long discussions with the surgeon the only option I had was yet another amputation. The thought petrified me and I didn't find it the case that the

more you have the more you get used to it – that's simply not true. Following the depressing all-day appointment I knew I couldn't dwell on it. I had to focus on my future and all the good things I hoped it would hold. Chris accompanied me back to London as he had a conference to go to.

I was still quite worried about London and almost had a phobia about going there. However, once I actually got there I found that I loved it. I had changed from the one-legged Cornish girl who was petrified of the place to an excitable one-legged woman who wanted to succeed in the world. I actually felt comfortable in London and despite the increase in numbers of people, I was actually stared at less. I felt like the real me for the first time in a long time.

The day of my meeting at Max Clifford's offices had arrived and I got to Bond Street three hours too early. How crazy is that? I wanted to show I was eager – but three hours too eager was ridiculous. I decided to go shopping. BIG MISTAKE! As I walked around Oxford Street in a suit, high heel and crutches with a heavy backpack I became increasingly exhausted. It was times such as this which made me realise how difficult things can really be. It was

tough being in a world where two legs would have been better than one. I wandered around the different stores trying to ignore the fact that I probably needed an oxygen mask and a seat!

I must have looked an absolute wreck as I arrived at my destination some three hours later. I had sweat pouring down my back and my make-up was running. I was extremely hot and my one and only ankle resembled a balloon. I took myself off to the café opposite where I rushed to the toilets in an attempt to try and make myself look more presentable. In the lift up to Max's office my stomach was doing somersaults and I had a mixture of feelings which made me undecided about whether I was more anxious or more excited. I was greeted by Louise who was lovely and some other staff and I looked at the framed photographs of Simon Cowell, Gillian MacKeith and Peter Jones on the wall while I waited. I realised they had all probably stood where I was now.

Max was exactly as I thought he would be. Strong, kind and intelligent and at that moment I decided that I wanted the life that I could have if I moved in his world. I wanted the buzz of London and the thrill of success. In

the meeting I explained about my vision, the DVD, and that I wasn't a wannabe. I was a somebody who worked hard to make things happen and I left the meeting feeling that I had made some progress. I knew that I had a big job to make the DVD work but I had promised him I'd be back with my product. Bouncing with success from the trip I couldn't stop thinking about the future. I could shrug off the ill health so that I could embrace a new life of success and excitement. But all thoughts of a better new life were suppressed for a time when I made the trip back to Stanmore. "One last time!" I told myself. I prayed that would be the case. After the operation I had a long time to lie in bed and think about my future. I had a little pink notebook for writing down my ideas and for planning the projects I yet wanted to achieve. It helped spur me on.

This time I met Jo at Stanmore who was going through her first amputation. I felt like an old hand and together we helped each other through. We were similar in several ways and although we would both cry with the agony we would also giggle like naughty school girls and it felt like destiny to be put in the next bed to her.

As well as the obvious down times in hospital the one

thing that hurt the most was that I missed Maisie's first birthday. I was gutted. Lying in my bed thinking of her was a sad time for me. I had bought her a big, pink inflatable ball pool and lots of other fun presents which I hoped she was enjoying on her very special day. I was an inpatient for two weeks and it took all my strength to get through. I had got used to seeing a new shaped stump following surgery and the staff were, as always, amazing, but it didn't ease the sickness, bleeding, needles, pain and rehabilitation that I went through. But, part of me felt different. I had so much to look forward to and I had many things to fight for. I had prospects, a life plan and I was going to get better no matter what life threw at me.

Mum had taken time off to help me get over the first few days at home which helped me and took the pressure off Paul – it also meant he came home to a cooked meal. Recuperating gave me time to plan and I wanted to get on with making the DVD. I had different medication which brought on some nasty side affects. Tamoxifen was a breast cancer drug but it might help me. Each day I took the pills and told myself it was doing me good despite the hot sweats and tiredness it gave me.

I wanted the DVD's location to be special. All other fitness DVDs seemed to be shot in white dance studios and I thought something more interesting would be good. Then it hit me – the Eden Project would be perfect. The more I thought about it the more ideal it seemed. I was Cornish, it was Cornish and it was also stunning. It had already played a big part in my life and I decided to approach Eden to see what they thought. Jo Gale said that Eden would be delighted – I was overjoyed at the news.

Everyone was excited as usual but whatever I had to say about my latest project wasn't shocking or surprising anyone anymore. I knew it would be a huge project but that was why I wanted to do it. Then I decided that Amanda and Angie, the only two women who had opened their classes to me would be perfect for the job. I was able to move a bit by then and took them out for a meal to discuss my ideas.

I ordered salad and a mineral water which I knew would make my friends laugh but – sitting opposite two fitness instructors – the steak and chips on the menu didn't seem appropriate. They were genuinely impressed with the idea and they both wanted to come on board. It was

summer and I had been attending aerobics once a week while working on the campaign for the project. I met Andy, a videographer from First Third Productions and he also seemed intrigued.

Working on the DVD made me realise that I now had a huge appetite for life and it was as if I couldn't get enough of it. I was on some kind of mission to savour every moment and I was spending time at work and in London where I met potential managers and agents. Don't laugh, but I signed on with a modelling agency but, at home, was being urged to relax sometimes. It was pointed out to me that I would jeopardize my health if I pushed myself too hard. But I'd turned a corner and I was determined to make the most of it. I was always quick to point out I was better but underneath it all the pain was still intense.

One weekend my entire family went for a relaxing break near Falmouth where the boys played golf and mum, Kate, Maisie and I swam in the pool and lay on sun loungers. It was fabulous and I actually did give my body a break. It also gave me some time with Paul which was something we'd been lacking for a while. We went for a swim and heard some people entering the pool area. We

were usually alone so I looked around to see who had arrived. I couldn't believe it because there in front of me was Des Lynam.

I played it cool as I casually said: "Hello." However, once he left the three of us were like gaggling girls as we jumped out and raced off to find the men in our lives – but there he was talking to them with his partner. Being football fans, Paul and I had watched him for hours on television and it was a bit surreal to suddenly be talking to him. We enjoyed a blissful weekend and I went out to the car in my electric wheelchair to pack it away when it was time to leave.

"Hello," said a voice behind me. It was him. We chatted before Paul joined us and neither of us felt star-struck talking to this amiable man. "Do you mind if I ask what happened to you?" he said in his sexy voice. I have always had a thing for older men – as you've probably gathered – and I'm sure Paul realised I was flirting with him as I told him my story. I reassured him as I did with everyone that I was okay and we wished him a pleasant journey home as we said our goodbyes. Paul and I got into the car and were talking excitedly about him and about

how lovely he was, but we were soon interrupted as he strode back towards our car. "Sorry," he said as he approached. "I was thinking…would you mind having my phone number…just call if you need anything."

Did I mind? Did I mind? He didn't need to ask twice. I couldn't believe the end to my lovely weekend. Later on, my parents received a call from the hotel. Des had asked if he could have my address. They agreed and then it was back to business as usual. Word had spread to the local media that I was preparing to make my own fitness DVD. I agreed to do a piece for ITV called *Inspirational Lives* where I demonstrated at a local gym in my not so glamorous tracksuit and bounced up and down on a fitness ball as I did an interview about the DVD. Des Lynam had done an interview at the *Countdown* studios in Leeds where he had talked about me as an inspiring person. I was over the moon as I gushed on television about my future with Paul – they'd heard on the grapevine we were planning to get married – and then I found myself nominated as Cornwall's Young Woman Of The Year. It was an incredible summer. I was dealing with more than I should have, as we'd been planning a wedding, preparing

to shoot a fitness DVD and I was holding down a day job. I was incredibly tired, but I continued all the same.

The wedding had been talked about ever since Paul proposed and by now we'd been together a long time. My wonderful grandparents insisted on buying me a wedding dress and we went off to buy one together. It took about two minutes as I fell in love with the first one I saw. We were accompanied by my parents and Charlie – as chief bridesmaid – and once again we were all crying! I felt like a princess.

It was all dashed when my health got worse again and I needed several weeks' intensive radiotherapy. I had known for ages I wasn't well but I've never been that good at listening to my body and I was incredibly stubborn. The one thing that brought me down was the one thing that kept me fighting. One day when I was alone I thought about the next few months and I was determined that the treatment would not end all my plans. I would pick myself up as I had done many times before. I lay on the sofa and enjoyed a rare moment of solitude watching the television. I noticed an advert for a new television show. It was an *Apprentice*-type show in which *Big Brother* star Jade Goody

was looking for a personal assistant.

The sane part of me told me to forget it. It wasn't a career move I wanted and I certainly wasn't well enough to go through with it, or was I? I mentioned it to my family and friends who thought that I'd be crazy to do it. That's when the insane part kicked in and I decided I had to apply. I crawled upstairs on my bum as I usually did and looked online. I filled in the application form and attached a CV and some photos as requested. I saw on another website that thousands of people had applied so to me I thought it was a bit of fun. After all, what would be the chances of me getting any further?

JUST A *Step*

Chapter 9

Showtime…!

As well as Amanda and Angie, I had also hired a fitness instructor called Lydia from London. The last thing I wanted was amateur rubbish so I knew I needed a professional. Amanda recommended her and as the preparations got underway I realised that I was taking on another huge financial gamble. Professional instructors, camera crews, production people, to name but a few of the things I needed, all cost money and I was soon using my credit card again. I did believe it would pay off though and the fact that I could end up with an inspiring product kept me going.

Radiotherapy was due to start and the increasing time spent on the DVD meant that Paul and I decided to postpone the wedding. The thought of putting granny's net curtains on my head reminded me that I wanted the perfect day and even though I could no longer walk down the aisle unaided or enjoy the first dance it was a difficult

decision not to go ahead. I felt as if I had let people down. Mum was devastated; she had already bought her hat. Dad being sensible understood our reasons and all four parents supported us fully.

It was especially hard telling my grandparents who had bought me the perfect dress. I felt guilty and family had been planning to travel from Australia. It was difficult not to feel bad, but it just didn't feel right. We agreed that marriage for us at that time wasn't going to be a good thing and we also agreed that I needed the radiotherapy to get better. I'm sure the saying "All good plans…" was invented when I was born because just then there was another crazy twist in the journey.

Totally out of the blue I received an email from a television production company to say that I had an audition for *Jade's PA*. I couldn't believe it as I shouted downstairs to Paul what the email said. I travelled to London on my own to sit in front a panel of judges and it was like being in a whirlwind. I was doubtful I'd get any further so I decided to treat it as "an experience." As my taxi pulled up outside the building where the auditions were being held I was half tempted to tell the driver to

drive off when I saw the huge queue that had formed. I confirmed in my mind I wasn't going to get any further. But I got out and decided to try my luck. We all stood outside in the rain for several hours and I was kindly offered a chair by the production crew. I didn't accept it and wriggled around on one foot like a lunatic. Once inside the hall it was like a scene from the *X Factor* and we were like cattle being herded around as we waited several more hours.

Back home I always thought I was the outgoing one – the loud, crazy one who was eccentric and who stood out for obvious reasons, but in that room I was totally invisible. People came from all walks of life and I soon noticed that every loud and crazy person was being handed an orange sticker while others were being given green, yellow and blue ones. I had my pre-interview with production and didn't know whether I should be pleased or offended when they stuck an orange sticker to my chest. Orange, though, meant that you were interviewed by Jade herself and a few minutes later that's exactly where I was – upstairs, sitting outside the room waiting to be called in.

"Leanne!" she shrieked in her distinctive accent as I

made my way down the stairs and sat in front of the panel. Once the interview was over I thought I had done well. I was asked about my disability and said honestly that it had never hindered my performance and that I gave 100 percent to any task I was set. Jade seemed nice but I was sure I hadn't made it through just by the sheer numbers there were applying. I was pleased though that I'd got out of the taxi earlier in the day. I made it back to Cornwall and a few days later received a call from Kate, the show's producer. "Pack your bags, Leanne...you're coming to London," she said. I had got through!

I wasn't sure if I was ecstatic or petrified. I hadn't thought I'd get this far and what had started out as a bit of fun was fast turning into reality. There was a mixed reaction from loved ones. Paul and my family were concerned for my health and some of them thought I was being stupid trying to attempt the show, but I wanted to prove to them I could manage it. After talking to everyone it was decided that I could go if the oncologist and specialist thought I was up to it, who said I should "go for it" and I began to cry when they told me I needed to enjoy the good things that I could do. They said they were

rooting for me. It gave me even more determination. I didn't have that long to organise myself and immediately booked leave from work and went shopping!

I woke up early on the morning I was due to go to London and found I was buzzing with every emotion possible – excitement, fear and anxiety – did I really know what I'd let myself in for? Mum called first thing to ensure I was awake, I didn't want to miss the train after all as that wouldn't have been a good start. I said my goodbyes on the phone to my parents who told me they would be unable to come to the station. I must admit I was quite sad that they wouldn't be there to wave me off – but it was a bit of a trek for them first thing in the morning so I told them both I loved them and that I'd see them soon.

I got ready and slipped into one of my outfits and was ready to "rock and roll". Chris came to collect Paul and me to take us to the station and it felt strange that I would be leaving them for a while. Even Maisie was coming with us and there she was in her car seat. I was glad I had the chance to be with my darling girl for the short car ride. As we pulled into Truro station, Paul and Chris were struggling with my suitcases and bags – well, they were

essential for a girl that was about to appear on a television show. We walked through the lobby and as we passed the photo booth I could hear familiar voices.

Yes, it was mum and dad who jumped out of the booth and threw their arms around me. I had quietly suspected that they wouldn't let me go without a big hug. I had my perfect goodbye. As we waited for the train I became more and more nervous. Chris put Maisie on my lap and she gave me a big cuddle. A cuddle, as you'll no doubt have realised, always made me warm inside. Even though she couldn't speak yet I'm sure she knew I was leaving and I felt incredible love for her.

As the train pulled in, right on cue, mum started to cry and before long we were virtually all in tears. It was happiness though and I was going on a big adventure and after all we had been through I was still here. I hugged everyone and gave Maisie, Kate and Chris big kisses. When I hugged my dad he just said: "I'm proud of you babes." It meant the world to me. I asked him to look after Paul as mum and I boarded the train. First Class – can you believe it?

Okay, so it was a weekend rate and I had been

upgraded for £10.00, but nevertheless, it all added to the excitement I was feeling, and dad and Paul quickly followed onto the train to put my suitcases and bags on behind me. I settled into my seat with my crutches close beside me. They all jumped off the train and as it started to move, I looked out of the window – and there they were – my life, my blood. I saw them in tears but I was feeling so very proud. I was also feeling extremely loved and I was starting out again in life – after such a long time of not much of a life. I waved as if I would never see them again and as I did I spotted Maisie waving back. That started the tears!

It felt like I was going on a school trip and I was buzzing inside as I made my way to the big smoke. The usual five-hour journey seemed to race by and before I knew it a kind man was helping me from the train with my bags. I hopped onto the mobility trailer and was delivered safely to the taxi rank. As usual I was greeted by a cheeky cabbie who wanted all the details about how I lost my leg. I answered all his questions and enjoyed the conversation. I even told him what I was doing in London and the mission ahead of me. I couldn't quite contain

myself – and I've never been that good at keeping things to myself.

As we arrived at the hotel I felt more and more nervous. I didn't know what other "characters" had got through the heats and who I'd be living with over the next couple of weeks. So, as I walked in, my eyes scoured the lobby like a hawk. The first person I saw was Emma – from Wales – who was there with her husband. We quickly got together and started nattering like two old ladies. We were wondering who else would be there. Not long after Emma, Becky arrived. Becky was from Liverpool – she was funky and had a great sense of style – and she was incredibly skinny (the cow). My face beamed as another contestant arrived. It was Tara. She had been someone who at first I had been wary of, she was self-confident and a little older than me, but I had quickly grown to like her and appreciated what an amazing person she was. Then to finish off our group of five, in walked Chantelle. I was also pleased that Chantelle had got through. She seemed kind and caring and I knew we'd get on.

The five of us got together that evening and nattered about the crazy things that might lay ahead. But we all

decided we were definitely in need of some beauty sleep as we wondered who we'd be meeting the next day. As I got to my hotel room I felt slightly homesick but tried to let it wash over me by choosing an outfit for the following day. I opted for black – for slimming purposes, of course – and a pair of killer heels, well, heel. I rang Paul and my parents filling them in on who had got through so far and all that had happened so far. I knew that they would be at home excited for me and I knew they were with me in spirit. As I lay in bed I wondered about the days ahead – had I really contemplated what would happen to me? Could my body take the physical side of it and would I be able to keep up with the others? All thoughts soon faded though when I drifted off to sleep. I was absolutely shattered.

"Bzzzzzzzz, Bzzzzzzzzz," the alarm shrieked around the room – I felt as if I'd only been asleep for a couple of hours. For once, I was keen to jump out of bed and ready to make myself look the most gorgeous that I possibly could, knowing that it was only a matter of time before I would face the cameras. I was upset to find that there wasn't actually a bath in my room, only a shower and while that would be great for anyone else simply wishing to grab

a shower and wash their hair, it wasn't that easy for me. The nerves crept in once again and I wondered if I was doing the right thing?

Anyway, moans aside, I found a way to wash myself and my hair and spent most of my time doing my favourite activity – applying my make-up. For once I had one of those really great hair days where it fell into place quite beautifully. I was certainly pleased with the end result. I must have looked in the mirror a thousand times until I was happy with my reflection and I was then ready to meet the other guys for our arranged breakfast down in the restaurant. As I made my way down in the lift, I saw my soon-to-be new housemates and everyone was "dressed to impress". We met in the lobby and once again we all began speculating on who else would be joining us to make the numbers up to 10. It wasn't long before our curiosity was satisfied as the remaining five contestants plus some of the film crew arrived.

Another Emma, who I had briefly met at the auditions, turned up. She was quite a quiet girl but friendly, and she was swiftly followed by Caroline. I hadn't met Caroline before but I found that I instantly liked her. She was

young, enthusiastic and just had a great aura around her. I warmed to her straight away and was pleased that we would soon be living together. We all talked about the fact that we were all girls and that we were surprised no boys had got through. But we were soon interrupted by Kate, the producer, who ushered us down to breakfast, leaving us to wonder about the other three who would be joining us. Downstairs we grabbed a table and ate toast as we continued to find out as much as possible about our rivals. Everyone around the table seemed to get on well and we were all quite girly talking about clothes, make-up and wondering what our new pad in London would be like. I suppose it was every emotion all round. Nervousness, excitement and anticipation, and for me personally, I had to ask myself the question: "Am I physically going to be able to do this without killing myself?"

Just then there was a lot of noise as the three remaining contestants arrived. To my delight, there were two more girls and a BOY! I thought that was great – it would certainly bring another dimension to the group. They included Zarah, from London – who I'd had doughnuts with at one of the previous auditions. The

lovely Jo, a fabulous older lady was fun and vibrant (and my kind of person) and the flamboyant and eccentric Eric – the token boy – who was definitely going to be fun. I felt confident with the 10 contestants that had been selected – there would certainly be lots of laughs.

We had a briefing at the hotel and each then had an individual meeting with the production crew. During my interview I was completely myself and I felt relaxed. I told them honestly that I was really excited about the show but that I didn't want any sympathy. I told them that I was nervous about whether I would cope physically, but I would certainly have a good bash at it. Following all the briefings we were all ushered into the waiting people carriers outside the hotel which had arrived to take us to our new "home". We were like children on a school trip all chatting like crazy and wondering what the next couple of weeks would bring. I was pleased that I was in the car with Emma from Wales and Chantelle – two people with whom I had immediately bonded. I suppose I hoped that they wouldn't "help me", but like my friends at home be aware of my situation. Maybe lend a hand, grabbing my crutches for me, etc.

We were taken to a very large and unique looking house in Finchley, North London and I felt like we were more like movie stars as we pulled up outside the house that looked like a film set with its cranes, cameras and lots of crew outside. The adrenaline was pumping and I didn't feel nervous, just excited. As the cars came to a stop, one of the producers, Tom, popped his head in the window and explained what we were going to be doing. It was simple, the car would pull up outside the house, we'd get out, stop, take a long look around, smiling all the way and then we would take our suitcases and make our way, in single file to the front door. All the time, the cameras would be rolling. That sounded simple enough.

As our car got into position around the corner, one thought went through my mind. "How the hell am I going to take my suitcase into the house?" It was big, bulky and heavy and there was no way I would manage it on crutches. Panic hit. As usual, I didn't want to be a pain and I didn't want to show any weakness immediately as I arrived! It sort of hit my confidence, I couldn't even carry a suitcase! In my panic, I spoke to Emma and Chantelle in the car and said that I was worried. I said it was something I

couldn't keep to myself and that I needed help – and quickly. Instantly, Emma said: "I've got a tiny case with a handle....you can carry that in, no one will ever know." I could have hugged her – what a great idea.

With military precision the cars pulled up, we got out, looked up at the house and took our cases in one, by one. No one seemed to question the fact I had the tiniest case on the planet and everyone watching at home would probably think "dirty cow" – it would have been pushing it to get 12 pairs of clean knickers in there – but I didn't care. It seemed to be one hurdle that I'd overcome. All ten smiles soon faded as we did the "entering the house" scene for about the tenth time. It always looked so simple and glamorous on the television, but I soon found out that nothing ever happened in one cut and had to be repeated again and again, until it was exactly right. As my ankle and foot began to swell in my new high-heeled black and while stiletto, all I wanted to do was sit down.

We finally made it into the house and as the cameras were turned off the crew brought all the rest of our bags in, including my two suitcases and a holdall stuffed with new shoes, outfits and copious supplies of ever-faithful make-

up – after all – it was television, darling. We had a quick look inside our new house which was extremely lavish. We had several more takes to do before the cameras finally stopped rolling. Everyone then ran for the stairs to grab the best beds while I continued to smile as everyone shot past me. I was left bringing up the rear, crutching my way up the stairs on my very uncomfortable heel. Thinking I'd be left with the dregs, I finally made it to the top of the stairs where I heard a voice say: "Leanne, we've saved this one for you." Emma and Chantelle had saved me a bed.

Emma was in the single bed and Chantelle and I were going to share the gigantic queen sized bed opposite. I was so grateful that they had included me and that I hadn't arrived at the bedrooms to find myself in the worst bed. I thought they were incredibly kind to look out for me and with such lovely people around I thought I'd get on just fine. It had been a long day – travelling to our new pad, meeting each other and forming friendships as well as filming our first takes for the camera. I was still thinking about having the world's smallest suitcase. Once again I felt like I'd only had two hours sleep when the alarm went off the following morning. I felt like a zombie. We had a

shower in the room's ensuite but it was obviously no good for me and probably a bit dangerous – having only one leg – but I didn't want to draw attention to myself. I was worried that making a fuss because I couldn't have a shower would give the other contestants the impression I was a pushover as that certainly wasn't the case.

When I got downstairs the house was a hive of activity. There were cameras set up and make-up artists waiting and there were people everywhere. I loved it. Our make-up was done which was a real treat for me and then we were ushered into the living room where Jade then made an entrance and "ACTION" was shouted on set. We were told in dramatic fashion that one of us would be leaving that evening. My heart was racing. How embarrassing would it be to have come all that way and get kicked out after one day? I didn't want to be evicted first. The challenge was to argue our case as to why we were best for the job. I'd got on with everyone well and thought, naively, that I was among friends. As I began my own case I was quickly interrupted by another contestant. "Leanne, I'm going to say what everyone is thinking...you are the weakest here as you cannot physically do the job like

everyone else." I was stunned. Feeling quite angry and without thinking my first word on national television was: "BOLLOCKS!" I'm sure if I'd had time to think I could have thought of something better, but this was a "dog eat dog" situation. I continued in a firm voice that whatever I was lacking physically I more than made up for mentally. I stuck up for myself. She was also quickly shot down by Jade and other judges and after more tests and challenges it was Emma that was evicted that night.

What had happened earlier stayed with me. I didn't want to cry and I wanted to appear strong and as I went to bed I took my pill box containing my Tamoxifen into the toilet. No one knew I was going to have to undergo more treatment or that I was taking pills and I wanted it to stay that way. I didn't want their sympathy, but I realised I was in a house with strangers and I had to stand on my own two feet – excuse the pun! As the days wore on I was more and more exhausted. We were up at 5.00am each morning and sometimes didn't get to bed until 3.00 am. Mornings were a race to the bathroom.

I'd managed to avoid eviction and I was pleased and strangely I was growing close to the woman who'd

ridiculed me in front of the cameras. She had been controversial, but she'd also said what she thought and I respected that. In the evenings between takes I was able to call home and I often cried down the phone because I was tired and I was struggling. But I wouldn't, couldn't, give up.

All the contestants were different but we did become quite close. Eric was a constant laugh and extremely outrageous. Tara had become a friend and she was very caring towards me. Caroline was really sweet and Jo, or Jo Jo as we called her and Zarah were like mums and I loved sharing with Chantelle and Emma. The only person I didn't particularly get on with was Becky but then no one else seemed to either.

My most memorable day came when I was evicted! We'd been completing different tasks around London and when I was able to relax, or rather collapse, I did. I'd already told some of the crew that I was really struggling and when Jade announced my name I was relieved. When the cameras stopped rolling she came over and hugged me and I went upstairs to pack my bags. "I'm honestly pleased I'm going," I said as I tried not to cry. I was

overcome with emotion and then it all came out about how I was going home to begin radiotherapy again. I cried.

I'd had time on the show and in the house to pretend there was nothing wrong with me and I'd pushed myself to the limit. I needed to go home to rest. I was driven to a hotel where I felt absolutely exhausted and I couldn't wait to get home. I took some days off when I finally made it back to do nothing but sleep. I had only been away for around two weeks but it felt like a lifetime and being home and holding Maisie was amazing. Each day there were ups and downs and I had to deal with them as they came along. Another twist came when Chris and Kate announced they were to part because they had decided they were better off without each other. It was sad, but there was still Maisie whom Chris and everyone else in the family adored. After a few days I went back to work and spent evenings working on my *Leanne's Chair Workout* DVD. I was back to living on adrenaline.

For 25 days I went to radiotherapy and I was sure that this time, along with the Tamoxifen and a positive attitude, it would work. I would kick it once and for all. I also let people help me more for the first time and most

days Charlie took me. As treatment came to an end, filming was about to start. I had to pull something from deep inside me to make it work – I had to – this was my future.

The two days we filmed in the biomes at Eden were a killer and I gave 100 percent to every scene. I got goose bumps when I saw *Leanne's Chair Workout* "Take One" written on a clapper board – it was an incredible feeling that more than made up for the sore backside I got from sitting in a wheelchair for two days. When I shouted: "It's a wrap!" at the end of filming it was an emotional moment but I now knew I had to sell the DVD and I couldn't wait.

The website was up and running and in the first week had received more than 26,000 hits. I was stunned. People from all over the world were ordering and paying for the DVD before it was even available. Andy was working hard on producing the DVD and I was hands on designing the cover and wording for the advertising and marketing. I'd never done anything like it before but it was exciting. I watched Andy put the DVD together and found it fascinating.

Costs were rising, but luckily, so were the sales and I

reeled off to Paul how many purchasers in different countries were buying it including people in Australia, Italy, Spain, Germany, the Czech Republic, France, the US – the list was endless. I was feeling incredibly proud. The success drove me forward once again and as the DVD was in the factory being produced I travelled up to London many times to meet potential distributors and managers.

On one of my trips I went to the finale party of *Jade's PA* in Leicester Square and met Russell Brand, the television and radio presenter. We chatted and afterwards we gave each other a kiss to say goodbye. It was all a bit surreal really. The following morning when I went back to work I got quite a shock when I picked up the phone and was asked: "Good morning Leanne. We would like to know if you would like to confirm what's in today's newspaper?" "Newspaper?" I enquired hesitantly. I went on to say that I couldn't comment on something I hadn't seen as one of my colleagues legged it to the newsagents.

We all gathered around my desk and turned the page to read "Russ' Brand New Gal" emblazoned across it directly above two pictures of us kissing in Leicester

LEANNE GROSE

Square. I hadn't expected to be in a national newspaper and as I explained to my mum, it was certainly an experience. It had given me more of a taste for the limelight and when the DVD arrived I cried with joy as I opened the first box containing the first 1,000 copies. Paul and I packed the orders ourselves and I put a personal note in with every one. The fact that people all across the globe were buying something I had created made me feel proud and it wasn't long before the letters started arriving.

I was overwhelmed by the responses. People loved it. Many said it was one of the best things they'd bought and that it was changing their lives for the better. Some, like me, were amputees while others had illnesses such as cerebral palsy, multiple sclerosis and cancer. Some had had strokes and others were overweight and wanted to exercise. Fit and healthy people were also buying it and I'd achieved what I'd set out to do: I had made a DVD suitable for everyone. As I am writing now I have a pile of letters beside me all of which I will answer. At the end of 2007, *Leanne's Chair Workout* went into shops and my stomach flips with excitement every time I think about it. I always keep my fingers and five toes crossed that things will go

JUST A *Step*

well but as often happens – with the good, comes the bad.

Not long ago I found another lump in my stump and I'm praying hard it's nothing to worry about. I've been back to Stanmore – which is a long gruelling trip in the back of an ambulance – to have some more tests and see more consultants and I'm due back shortly for the results. I reason that by now I should expect the unexpected. Whatever the outcome I'm determined to continue my crazy adventure and who knows what 2008 will bring?

What I do know is that I'm going to make the most of each second and live for today. I was also signed up to write this book which has also been an amazing experience. Who would have thought that anyone would be interested in the story of a one-legged girl from Cornwall? But maybe that's a question you can answer!

"I assumed when I first met Leanne that she had been in a car accident, little did I know that she'd had several tumours which resulted in her having her leg amputated which was very sad - except I was the one that was sad as she certainly wasn't. I wish her all the best for a successful future." **Des Lynam**

"Leanne is one of those rare people of whom you can say, when they walk into the room, the room feels better for it. Her energy, vitality and sheer love of life shine through everything she does. Perhaps her health and her battle to keep it have provided the feisty edge which makes her savour it all the more. Her charisma and talent have raised awareness not only of her condition but that of many others, but unlike most others there isn't even a whiff of self pitying indignation or backward looking. To steal from The Police song 'Every little thing she does is magic...'. Give her your support for the best of all reasons, not because she asks for it but because you sincerely want to give it." **Tim Smit, Author and Creator of the Eden Project**

"After reading your story I have now decided to try and be as positive as you and get fit. I just really wanted you to know how you have helped me decide to make changes in my life, and live life to the full like you do. Absolutely fantastic, great fun and perfect for the wheelchair. Thank you so much for what you are doing and being brave enough to speak out for disabled people everywhere." **Sharon Bowie, United Kingdom**

"Leanne... You did a wonderful job demonstrating each and every Chair Workout routine in a very energetic and upbeat manner throughout your whole DVD... It was very motivational, inspiring and fun... It brought a smile to our faces while exercising... We wish that everyone disabled or not, could view it ..." **Diane and Don from Ohio, U.S.A.**

"Leanne is beautiful in heart and soul. Her unwavering positivity and genuine kindness are rare, special and totally uplifting." **Susie Carter, Journalist**

"You are a breath of fresh air! As a disabled person myself and very overweight I thought people gave up on the likes of us regarding exercise so it was a surprise to see your web site. The Americans seem to cater for larger people and those with disabilities but we here in the UK have been behind as usual. It is refreshing to see a young person going for it-and I wish you the best health and happiness for your future." **Deborah Hard, United Kingdom**

"The energy and enthusiasm shown by Leanne throughout all her endeavours is incredibly infectious and an inspiration to disabled and non-disabled people alike. On deciding to produce a Cyber Coach system for teaching fitness classes to groups of children, we spent months distilling which characteristics a performer should have to appear on the machine. We needed inspirational people with energy, enthusiasm, a constant smile, and warmth. Leanne possesses all of these, and many more, by the bucket load." **Glen Jones, Product Director, Cyber Coach**

WE SUPPORT FAMILIES
WE FIGHT INEQUALITY
WE MAKE COFFEE
WE RUN MARATHONS
WE FUND NURSES
WE PROVIDE GRANTS
WE GIVE OUR TIME
WE CHANGE LIVES

WE ARE MACMILLAN. CANCER SUPPORT

**We're all affected by cancer.
We can all help.
www.macmillan.org.uk**

Please visit:

www.justastep.co.uk